Newcastle

City Council

Newcastle Libraries and Information Service

☎ **0845 002 0336**

Due for return	Due for return	Due for return
....		....
....		....
....		....
....		....
....		....
....		....
....		....
....		....
....		....
....		....
....	....	....

Something About Women

P. H. Newby

Something About Women

André Deutsch

First published in Great Britain in 1995 by
Andre Deutsch Limited
106 Great Russell Street, London WC1B 3LJ

Copyright © P. H. Newby 1995
All rights reserved

The author has asserted his moral rights

ISBN 0233 98911 0

Printed in Great Britain by
W B C Bridgend

For Katie

Something about women troubles
Even old men and unicorns.
When will the nightingales return
And sing in the greenwood?

From the anonymous Persian
(16th century?)

1
Owen

The time had come round for writing his monthly article on religious affairs for *The Courier* and as usual he felt tense. He knew roughly what he was going to say but not how to say it so he went for a walk to see whether the exercise would prompt a few phrases. If he could get the first paragraph in his head the rest would follow. The ordination of women in the Church of England was his subject. All very tricky. Women were different from men, he wanted to say, but how could he do that in a way acceptable to Women's Lib? He did not want to be accused of male chauvinism.

The Reverend Owen Bark had been told by his GP, and more authoritatively by his sister Eleanor, not to expose himself to the cold. So he, an Emeritus Fellow of St Ebbe's College, should have known better than to go walking in the Botanic Gardens that bright and bitter winter afternoon. The snow was so dazzling he wished he had brought his dark glasses. The great willow, the Salix

Babylonica, was a favourite with him not only because of its elegance because he never saw it without thinking of the exile by the waters of Babylon and here it was, rooted in what had once been the Jewish graveyard. The tree was mis-named because it did not come from Mesopotamia at all but Owen did not care; it looked Babylonian to him and undoubtedly it was nourished by Jewish bones. It rose out of the snow with pyrotechnic flamboyance. If you could imagine anything so absurd as black fire.

The cold was bad for his heart but was there anything so glorious as a snowy garden in sunshine? Could not so much delight to the eye make up for the chill? Except for himself the garden seemed deserted. On the gravel paths the snow had melted but on the lawns it remained immaculate. No one had been there but the birds. Their tracks caught the light so that as he walked the snow gave off puckers of iridescence.

Mustn't overdo it. His breath hung gauzily in the air and he moved his scarf up to cover his mouth and nose. The heavy grey overcoat bought from Oxfam must have belonged to a shorter man because it did not come down to his knees. If only he had thought to put on his thermal long johns his legs would probably not be, as they now were, trembling. He felt quite wobbly.

But in the plant house it was gloriously warm. Palm trees rose in the humid brightness, fronds and leaves were in sweat and a strange-looking tree carried one large globular fruit, just dangling there and waiting for the predator, man or monkey, who must surely come. Owen removed his woollen cap, slackened his scarf and would have dipped his hand in the water where the lilies grew but for the sudden feeling someone had crept up behind him and was pushing gently but firmly between his shoulder blades.

There was no one behind him. He looked to see. The pressure became firmer. Inexorable, he thought. And with the pressure, between his shoulder blades, came shortness of breath as though his lungs were squeezed by this pressure, so much he might not be able to draw breath at all. If he stood still all might be well. It did not work. By now the pressure in his back had become a real ache and the lack of air made him clutch his throat. The heat was choking him and feeling helpless now he sat down, his legs forked, his back against one of the little walls that enclosed the plant beds thinking how strange he would look to anyone who came by, as surely someone soon would. They might think he was drunk.

From time to time he had attacks like this and knew that if he did not panic and took one of his tablets all would be well. First of all the pain in the back would go, his shallow breathing would slow and deepen, his body would lose its tension and his hands – which were now so clenched he could not have opened the bottle of tablets even if he had been able to get at it – would slacken.

'You O.K. then?' A youngish woman in jeans and an outsize jumper with Mickey Mouse on the front was looking down at him and Owen could only look back. All he could manage was a groan. This young woman had a lot of frizzy hair and one hand stuck into it as though she was holding her head on. It was difficult to be sure about the sex of some of these young people but he was sure she was a woman because she had that sort of voice and no bristles on her chin.

'Tablets. Inside pocket.' He jerked out these three words and even managed a gesture. She was extraordinarily quick to cotton on, bent down and thrust a hand inside his coat and jacket where he hoped she would locate the bottle in his right hand waistcoat pocket. Instead, she discovered his wallet inside a pocket of the jacket itself and extracted it as if relieving him of something he wanted to be rid of anyway. She had the self-satisfied air of one performing a much-needed and appreciated service. Then, stuffing the wallet inside her jumper she made off, closing the door noisily behind her, leaving Owen more amazed than angry in spite of his physical distress. Robbed! And by a woman! It was against nature.

A group of schoolchildren with notebooks and pencils now came in to be addressed sharply by a rough-looking man in a track suit who must have been their teacher. He caught sight of Owen sprawled in the corner and frowned in a way that showed he considered this no sight for his charges.

Owen managed to wave a hand. He croaked, 'My wallet. Gone.'

'What's that?'

'At least thirty pounds. And Visa card.' Owen tried to struggle to his feet and the schoolmaster went to help. Owen tried to wave him away with the result that he fell back, hitting his head against the wall. But this was not where he felt the pain. A shiver went through his whole body.

The schoolmaster picked on one of the boys. 'Go over to the office and get them to ring for an ambulance. This gentleman needs some proper attention.' He sent the rest of the children out of the plant house and posted himself at the door to prevent anyone from coming in.

'It's the police I want.'

All the windows of the plant house were fogged over except on the side of the enclosed passageway and out there Owen could see a climbing plant with white flowers that seemed to smile at him from some paradise too remote to be housed. He was gazing across continents.

'It's starting to snow again.' The schoolmaster had been outside and this is what he came back to report. 'The ambulance men are usually pretty quick. They'll see you O.K., sir.'

'The bottle. If you could get it out and give me a tablet.'

The schoolmaster did not want to get involved. 'Of course, the weather might hold them up.'

Eleanor would be furious when she learned that he had been out in this weather and brought on one of his attacks. Fortunately she lived out of town and would not learn of his misadventure until he chose to tell her. With a bit of luck there would be no need.

'Funny thing,' said the schoolmaster, 'I was involved in an accident only a week ago. The ambulance was on the spot within minutes. Ah! What was that?' He went outside again and returned with flakes of snow on his hair and shoulders. 'It'll be here any minute. I could hear the siren.'

'Take me to the police station.' When the ambulance men came in with a stretcher this was the first thing Owen said to them. 'Robbed. Just when I was helpless. And by a woman.' What Eleanor might say about that would certainly be upsetting.

The ambulance men took no notice. They lifted Owen on to the stretcher, stuck his hat on the back of his head, wrapped him in blankets and, after some difficult manoeuvering through the doors, carried him into the cold air where the sun had gone, the air bit and the snow fell steadily. They trundled him out of the main gate and into the warm ambulance where his face was so cold he disentangled an arm to rub his frozen nose. He was sorry he had left without thanking the schoolmaster but the ambulance man who stayed with him said that was O.K., the bloke would understand there was no time for frills in an emergency. No, they couldn't take him to the police

13

station. They could not take him home either. It was against regulations. There was only one place they could take him and that was to Casualty at the hospital where they would soon put him to rights.

About this the ambulance man had made no mistake. Within minutes of being wheeled into Casualty reception Owen was stripped of his outer clothes, put in a white gown and told to lie on a bed where a young woman who looked curiously like the one who had lifted his wallet proceeded to examine him. She was in a long white jacket and had a stethoscope hanging from her neck so presumably she was a doctor. She asked what had happened, took his blood pressure and gave instructions for an oxygen mask to be slipped over his nose. This was getting out of hand. He was perfectly all right. No pain in his back now and his breathing was back to normal. It had just been one of his attacks and if only the ambulance men had taken him home he could have been at work on his *Courier* article.

He gathered he was to be sent up to a ward. He had imagined he would be into Casualty and then straight home again. Not so. He would be there overnight at least and that meant word would have to be got to Eleanor. He was afraid of her and that was the truth of the matter. She, two years the elder, had dominated him since childhood and when, as now, he knew there would be another scene he thought of the birthday present disaster of – when was it? – fifty, no sixty years before. No doubt there were other humiliations he had forgotten but this one over the birthday present stuck in his mind. After war, after marriage, after the usual disasters of life and the occasional triumph, the row over Mama's birthday present still grumbled away.

He had decided to give Mama a sunshade with a green lining very like the one sported by a young woman in a French painting he had seen. It was a summery painting. Light, fleecy clouds moved in the bright sky. Behind her on the meadow bank was a boy in a hat who might have been Owen himself, just as the young woman might have been Mama, she was so like her. She looked out of the painting. Her gaze was steady, intimate and loving just as Mama's always was. Mama was the most beautiful lady in the world and he wanted her to have a sunshade too. She would carry it on the beach at their next seaside holiday and he would be so proud of her, looking so young, so radiant and so happy that he would want to rush up to people, to complete strangers, and say, 'That lady is my Mama.'

Eleanor had a different idea. Mama was Welsh and came from Bangor so when Eleanor saw a Victorian steel engraving of the Menai Bridge in a junk shop she decided nothing could be more appropriate. The trouble was it cost £8 and this was more than she could afford; but if Owen and she put their money together it would be just enough to buy the engraving. She took Owen to the shop. No, he thought it was a bad idea. He hated the dreary engraving. It had no colour. In any case he wanted to give Mama his own present as a way of showing how much he loved her. It was impossible to convey this to Eleanor who just enthused about Mama's predictable delight over the Welsh picture and Owen could not find the words to disagree convincingly enough.

This would have meant describing the young woman in the French picture and the way her face was in shadow. How could he say he wanted to see Mama, like this lady, out in the sunshine with a green-lined sunshade. So Eleanor never knew what his own choice of a present would have been. She bullied the four pounds out of him and the steel engraving of the Menai Bridge was what they jointly gave. To be honest, Mama was pleased with it. She hung it in her bedroom where she said it would remind her of old times but Owen never saw it without a pang.

Eleanor had a habit of telephoning soon after six o'clock when the cheap rate started but before that he wanted to ring her, explain what had happened and ask her to bring his note-book so that he could make a start on drafting that confounded article. He had been X-rayed, given an electro-cardiograph and heard talk of putting him on a treadmill which was a way of testing how much his heart could stand. It was most vexing. The hospital had contacted Flavers his GP to ask for his medical records. They made it sound quite a long job so he'd have to ask Eleanor to get his pyjamas and shaving gear as well as the notebook. She had a key to the flat. Once in the ward he made a nuisance of himself until a portable telephone was wheeled to his bed and coins fished out of his trouser pocket for him to slot in.

If it had not been for the stolen wallet Owen would have lied to Eleanor and said he had been taken ill at home but she would need to know where and how it had been taken so that she could report the theft to the police. He was right about her being annoyed. She seemed more concerned about the missing Visa card than anything else.

'Oh, Owen! You out on a day like this with the snow half way up the front door. Driven by the wind. It's like the Arctic out there. Do you mean you walked all the way to the Botanic Garden? That's really too much. How can you have been so stupid? Don't you ever think of me?

16

You don't know the number of your Visa card? Isn't that typical! How can I get it stopped if I don't know the number. The thief will be mulcting you of hundreds of pounds. I'm sorry to say this, Owen, but it serves you right.'

Eleanor could not believe that his attack had been so bad he was too feeble to put up any resistance to the thief. The police would not find the information about the Mickey Mouse jumper at all helpful. Finally, there was no question of her turning out on a night like this to pick up stuff from his flat. The roads would be impassable.

'Would you tell Mrs Springer?'

'The char? Oh, all right. Give me her number. But she's a dead loss that woman. She wouldn't even register you were missing.'

In spite of the chatter going on in the ward Owen tried to think about his *Courier* article. He was against the ordination of women in the Church of England not for the reasons that were ordinarily given but for tenuous reasons hard to put into words. He attached little importance to the view that the Anglican ordination of women would make re-union with the Roman Church more difficult because he saw little merit in that anyway. For years he had considered the ecumenical movement misguided. What purpose would it serve other than uniformity and was it not in the very nature of religious belief in the modern world that in uniformity lay dissidence and, if not dissidence, hypocrisy? He did not attach much importance either to the fact that Jesus was male and all his disciples were male too. No, what Owen wanted to say was something profound about the relationship between men and women, between maleness and femininity, something that D. H. Lawrence would have understood and, if only Owen could find the passage, had probably

17

already said. Owen had, however, such a distaste for the writings of D. H. Lawrence that he could not expose himself to the reading that would be required.

A nurse who had just come on duty was full of news about the weather. A real blizzard out there. She had been lucky to get in herself but that was because she lived really local and had been given a lift in one of the ambulances. Incredible. It was like Siberia. According to a chap on the radio Banbury was cut off.

Eleanor must have found out which ward he was in because she telephoned that evening. The ward sister brought the message which was that conditions were really bad. Two cars were in the ditch just outside her cottage and one of the drivers had been in to phone for help. She could not see herself getting out of the village for days. Did Owen know anyone living near the hospital who could bring him what he wanted?

'There's Arthur Minchin. He lives in Sandford Road. But I don't want him bothered, not in this weather.'

Owen offered Arthur up in this sacrificial way because otherwise Eleanor would have made it her business to phone round his other friends until she located somebody who would probably be less fit. Arthur was a man who had refereed what he called 'coarse rugby' until he was well into his fifties, a rugged man who would look on a little local blizzard as an agreeable challenge. At least Owen hoped so.

He asked the ward sister to say he expected to be out of hospital in a day or two so there was no need to make demands on Arthur or anyone else for that matter.

The ward sister came back. 'She sends her love.'

Love? Yes, that was a word that would come into his article if only he could handle it aright. The Greeks called it *agapé*. What did it mean nowadays, love? To most

18

people it meant just sex. Yet there was no other word to express the feelings we should all have for each other, more particularly the feeling men should have for women and women for men, than love. But it could not be slipped into a newspaper article as easily as all that. It would need the most delicate presentation. Eleanor's use of the word had not made it any easier.

The ward was so hot Owen slept in his underclothes without any covers and enjoyed the deepest sleep, and the most vivid dream, in the moments before being awakened by the breakfast trolley. The snow had petered out, the wind had dropped and by the time Arthur Minchin came in the sun just glared through the windows.

'You look all right. I expected to see you in bed.'

'Oh, I got dressed. I had this dream. I dreamed about Margaret. It wasn't any ordinary dream, Arthur. It was so vivid.'

'Who's Margaret?'

Owen was amazed. 'You remember Margaret.'

'Sorry.' Arthur had brought a battery operated shaver, a tooth brush, paste, towel, hair brush and comb. 'Your sister seemed worried. But women always exaggerate; wouldn't have come so sharp if I'd known you were up and about. The snow's all frozen. Cars all over the place.'

Arthur had worked on the catering side in the Bursar's office before he retired and Owen thought he had been there for years, certainly long enough to remember Margaret.

'Margaret. My wife, Margaret.'

Arthur shook his head. 'Never had the privilege. Didn't even know the name. It was all sort of hush-hush, wasn't it?'

Having one of his attacks, being robbed in the plant house and then being shunted off to hospital must have confused Owen more than he realised because he could have sworn Arthur not only knew Margaret but was quite a buddy of hers. This involved counting the years. It had been twenty, no twenty-five years – God! was it so long? – since Margaret walked out on him, taking Charlotte with her. It had been just such another winter as this one promised to be, 1963 could it be, or maybe earlier, when there was snow on the ground from just after Christmas until late March. They had moved into the Summertown house, the one with the huge garden, where it was not until Easter and the ice and snow had melted that they discovered paved footpaths out there they had not suspected.

Arthur said he did not come to the college until 1972. He'd been with British Rail before that, supervising the dining cars that operated from Paddington. 'The Michael-mas term, 1972, it was. Even then the cars were being phased out. Didn't pay. People took sandwiches.'

Hush-hush? Yes, Owen supposed it was. The Master had been very kind. Everybody had been very kind. The Bursar's assistant, he now remembered, was a man who had served in the Army Catering Corps and that had been the talking point between him and Margaret, her father having been in the army too, a war-time major who wore a lot of medals at their wedding. He liked being referred to as the Major. The Bursar's assistant, name of Ingrams, had been a warrant officer in the Catering Corps and his attitude to the major's daughter had been respectful to the point of deference. And this pleased Margaret. When she unbent it was as a great lady being chatty with one of the tradesmen.

Normally, Owen did not dream. At least, he did not have dreams he could remember much about after waking up so what happened in the early hours of that morning was all the stranger. The man in the bed opposite made strangled cries in his sleep. This brought Owen to a dozey awareness, then he must have dropped off again because this is when he had the vivid dream about Margaret. She was in a pink light and her chubby face looked healthy, too healthy like a photograph in some holiday brochure. But the background was not a ski slope or the blue sky but the deck of an ocean-going liner with a funnel and deck chairs. She was wearing an evening dress which sparkled as she moved. Her hair, as it had always been, was cut in that neat way that lifted if off the back of her neck – she had always spent a lot of money on her hair – and what with the familiar smirk and the tilt of her head, chin up, she looked pleased with herself. Radiant was the word. He asked why she was dressed like that and she said the Hunt Ball was being held on the QEII that year. She had always loved dancing. He never did.

That was all. He must have made a move towards her because when he came to he was standing in the middle of the ward in his underclothes. He had got out of bed, made a few steps in his sleep and ended up, with arms extended, facing a nurse who seemed unsurprised. Just about any behaviour could be expected of patients. In his confusion he saw her as, in some way, a version of Margaret.

'Hunt Ball? Do you really have to go?'

'No way, Owen,' said the nurse. 'I'm not dressed for it.'

'I must have been dreaming.'

The radiant image of Margaret remained with Owen as he talked with Arthur about QMS Ingrams and the bad winter of '63. The hospital reminded him, a bit, of an ocean liner. Its long corridors could have been on board ship. Seen from a distance the low hospital building with smoke rising from a chimney looked curiously like a liner and this memory had probably sparked part of Owen's dream. But why had Margaret appeared so vividly? It was years since he had last heard from her, from Pittsburgh to invite him to Charlotte's wedding.

He always regretted not going. He ought to have gone and 'toughed it out' as the new phrase had it but Margaret had written such brutal letters about his refusal to divorce that he could not risk the possibility of a verbal assault, delivered in person, and no doubt abetted by that nuclear physics professor she was then living with. She subsequently divorced Owen in some American state where such charades were permitted and then went through what Owen thought of as an empty ceremony with this man. So far as Owen was concerned it counted for nothing. For him divorce after a Christian marriage was impossible. He and Margaret were married until 'death did them part.' It suddenly struck him that this is what the dream meant. Margaret had died.

It was wrong to allow so absurd an idea even to cross his mind. He had heard of such coincidences but did not believe in them. Just crude superstition. Pagan, almost. Or was it? Was it so very unChristian to believe in the paranormal?

'I'm Harman Phelps, Mr Bark.' The man was marked out from everybody else because he wore an ordinary suit. He had a close and carefully trimmed beard and a jaunty, rather naval manner to go with it. With him were a couple of medics in training whom Dr Phelps introduced before examining Owen's fingers. 'Haven't I seen you before, Mr Bark? Yes, I thought so.' He looked at some notes, an X-Ray and what Owen knew was an EC graph. 'You came in as an emergency.'

'I feel much better now and would like to go home.'

'Oho! Oho! We'd better hang on to you for a bit.'

'I take it I can always discharge myself.'

'That wouldn't be wise.'

With which Dr Phelps and his entourage swept on, the curtains that had been pulled round Owen's bed were drawn back and Arthur who all this time had been waiting said he had been down to the hospital shop and bought one or two things; a notebook, a ball-point and the *Daily Telegraph*.

'That was thoughtful of you. Could you lend me some cash? I need coins to feed that phone.' Owen hesitated. 'I'd appreciate it if you forgot what I said about Margaret. I wouldn't like my sister to know.'

'Oh, sure. Odd you should think I'd been in the college as long as all that. I ran into Mr Ingrams only the other day.'

'I wouldn't want him to know either.'

Fortunately Owen still had his diary in which he had noted important telephone numbers, so with the cash Arthur lent him he was able to call the Features Editor at *The Courier* and explain what was happening.

'Oh, hell!' Gladdy Walsh was a Scot and sounded it. 'That's all it needed. You say you've got it all in your head. Just go ahead. I could get one of the girls here to take it down.'

Owen said he could not work like that. He needed to see the stuff on paper so that he could tinker with it. Perhaps he had been exaggerating when he said he had it all clear in his head. What he was trying to say was very subtle and he did not want to be misunderstood; he was anxious not to give the impression he was against women. Just the opposite. He had to keep feeding the phone with coins and was aware that other patients in the ward were listening with interest. There was a Pakistani woman who never ceased from complaining that she had been put in a mixed ward. Owen did not mind her because she hadn't enough English to understand what he was saying but there was a fat man whose ears seemed to twitch with curiosity.

'Did you say you were in hospital, Owen? Sort of missed that. There's a lot of chaos going on here. Got to go.' And he put the phone down.

Owen called the police to check that the theft had been reported by Eleanor and found that it had. He found himself in conversation with a sergeant who had views on the rise of female crime. A young woman taking the wallet of a helpless man would have been unheard of when he started in the force. But nowadays? Female crime was the coming thing and that meant more women police officers. Women were taking over. When Owen was up and about again perhaps he would pop into the station and make a proper report. No, there had been no sighting of a woman in a Mickey Mouse jumper but she did not sound like a student. More likely somebody who needed the money for pot. Taking some drugs reduced the resistance to cold and that was why she had come into the plant house.

It had not occurred to Owen that his robbery by a woman might be worth mentioning in his article. Women were, quite rightly, taking over and up to a point Owen was all for it. For all too long women had a rough deal. They had been much put upon, treated as inferior, exploited, discriminated against and, when not regarded as nuisances, treated as so much property. No wonder they rebelled, no wonder they said they were as good as men if not better. But that was not to argue that they were the same as men.

This was when the woman doctor who had seen him when first he came into Casualty appeared and said his sugar count was high and he wasn't to be worried about this but he might be diabetic. His attack had been a shock to his system and might have brought it on. So he was to cut out as much sugar as possible and take some tablets. A sign saying 'Diabetic' was placed over his bed to warn the women who brought his food round not to give him any pudding.

Owen had adopted a new pattern of prayer, one week of what he regarded as the usual prayers followed by a week of non-prayers. By non-prayers he meant the making of his mind blank and exposing it to whatever God willed. Sometimes nothing happened at all and Owen was left feeling inadequate; at others he found himself exposed to reproaches and exhortations which were so unsettling it was not easy to fall asleep afterwards. But now he could not remember whether he was in a week of praying or of non-praying; that was some measure of the disorientation brought on by his attack. Non-praying was the more challenging endeavour so he decided that was what he would go in for, lying in his bed in the evening while the rest of the ward was busy around him, the very few visitors who defied the snow coming and going, the noise of the television in the corner, the swish of the curtains from time to time around the individual beds, the food trolley, the nurses talking quietly as they administered pills, bed pans, took blood pressures and temperatures. None of all this bothered Owen. He lay there with his eyes closed, saying, 'I am empty. Fill me.'

The message came through fitfully, interrupted not by the ward noises but by spiritual static. Now he could hear, now he could not. He did not deceive himself into thinking there was a real splutter of interfering sound; the deficiency lay in his own receiving mechanism, in whatever corresponded spiritually to a physical ringing in his ears. Interrupted and distorted though it was, the message was that he lived too much for himself, he was self-centred, indifferent to the troubles and anxieties of others. Not troubles in the wide world. He had a clear conscience about those. He helped in fund raising for Christian Aid, he had organised the sending of postcards to the President of Brazil protesting about child murder on the streets of Rio, he had even been on a sponsored bicycle ride to as many as thirty churches in the area to raise money for church restoration. His indifference and selfishness were more profoundly rooted. He just lacked the capacity of going out of his way to be nice to people. They did not feel cheered by his presence. He had failed in one of the important Christian duties, that of spreading happiness.

Such thoughts kept him awake. There was a Moslem saying he had once heard on the radio, that prayer was better than sleep, and whenever he thought of it and the monks and the muezzins who bore witness to it he was both consoled and concerned. Yes, he had always tried to pray well and there were times when it made him happy; more often though he might have done better. Or, when he was non-praying, when his receiver might have been more efficient. But there, in hospital, it seemed to be working all right. He was learning truths about himself he would have preferred to push aside. He hadn't enough love for people.

'I didn't know you was in 'ere, Rev.' The big man with blue eyes was not immediately recognisable without the straw boater he was usually seen in but it was the butcher Owen patronised in the covered market. 'Just visiting the wife. Varicose veins. And I 'appens to look in 'ere and who do I see but you. What's this?' He saw the notice over Owen's bed. 'Diabetic! 'Allo then! My old uncle 'ad the diabetics and d'you know what 'appened to 'im? They 'ad to saw 'is leg orf. Har! Har! Har!'

Everybody but the Pakistani woman joined in the laughter, especially the man with the twitchy ears. Owen laughed too.

'That was a long time ago, I expect. Before insulin.'

'Mind you, 'e lived a good while after that. 'E didn't think it was all that funny, 'aving 'is leg orf. 'E couldn't understand why we laughed. Well, it's life, isn' it? Tell you what, Rev. You're best in 'ere out of this weather. I couldna got in but I've got this Nip four-wheel drive.'

'Could you get me home?'

'You coming out, then? Where d'you live? Sure I could get you there all right.'

Owen went to the ward sister's desk and said he was checking himself out. He felt all right and he had important work to do. No doubt they would be glad of the bed.

The sister's name tab identified her as Shirley and she was merry about his threatened departure. 'Like that, is it? Had enough of us. The supervisor will be real upset.'

Getting out of hospital was not so easy. Owen had to be seen by the consultant, the dietician and the pharmacist and all this took so much time he had to send the butcher away. What clinched his departure was they really did need his bed and by early evening he was back in his flat with a new supply of tablets, an appointment with the heart clinic in a month's time and one with the diabetic clinic in six weeks. He also had instructions on diet. Very good service. Even the food in hospital had been edible. In one of his articles he'd say a good word about the NHS.

The butcher, who had driven out again to fetch him, produced a piece of fillet steak as a coming home present and would not leave until he had checked the heating. Such kindness made Owen feel weepy. Not only was he failing in love he was signally failing to count his blessings. Whatever his own inadequacies God's love was inexhaustible. It did indeed fill his cup to overflowing.

If Margaret was not dead had she been trying to get in touch? A letter to the old address could have been sent on but there was no knowing how many times the house had changed hands since he sold it. More likely Margaret had written to the college. He started with the porter. No, there was no mail for Mr Bark and he could remember none. Owen even spoke to the Master who said no one had used him as a forwarding address. The absence of some signal from Margaret began to seem stranger than the vivid dream. He had to shrug off what was becoming an obsession and the best way to do that was through work. On that article.

The ordination of women was an issue that would not have been raised with such urgency but for the current heresy that men and women were the same and interchangeable. They were not. They were different not only in the obvious way – women could not be fathers, men mothers – but in their souls. Men must work and women must weep. That was one way of putting it. Another would be to say that men were more aggressive, women more compliant. That was only one part of the story. No man is an island, no woman either; to be properly human each needed the other so that they might jointly aspire, however imperfectly, to be in the image of God. Without the love between men and women there could be no conception of that greater love. This love was expressed in the central act of Christian worship, the blessing by the priest of bread and wine so that they became for the worshippers the body and blood of Christ. The Eucharist could be mediated only by a man, not by a woman. Otherwise it would cease to express the binary nature of

28

the human psyche in which two souls like twin stars revolved round their common centre.

Owen hesitated. As this point it occurred to him the argument did not hold if the priest was a woman ministering to a male communicant. But no. This is where one had to remember that the rite was more mysterious. The priest was standing in for Christ who, as man and God, now presented himself to his church, as a man might present himself to his bride. The maleness was of the essence.

It was all proving more difficult than he had thought. Something was not quite right. After a rough draft he normally went for a walk to clear his mind but the weather made that impossible. From his window he could see a great tongue of iced snow hanging from an adjoining roof. He had to switch on the electric convector heater to supplement the radiator, it was that cold. Perhaps the pills made him more susceptible to cold; it numbed not only his hands and feet but his mind too. It turned not to some imagined female principle that needed cherishing but to real women he had known, even the one in the Mickey Mouse jumper; more especially it turned to Eleanor who, thank God, was still unable to visit him because of the weather. And most especially, it turned to his wife Margaret. In the dream she had appeared as he last saw her all those years ago, not a bit older, her face unlined. That must indicate something. She was a memory not a living presence. She was not trying to get in touch and the vision had been nothing more than the fantasy of a sick man.

He had forgotten another woman in his life, the elderly Mrs Springer who came in three mornings a week to clean and – as the mood took her – to cook his lunch. She lived near and came in spite of the Arctic conditions to give him, as he expected, a ticking off.

'I came in, Mr Bark, and finding you not 'ere was a real shock. If it 'adn't been for your sister phoning I don't know what I'd 'ave done. 'Ow are you, then? All right?' She was a small, easily angered woman. 'Still, it was better than finding you 'ere lying stretched out dead, as I said to my 'usband an' that. That did 'appen to a friend of mine – '

'Oh, please, Mrs Springer.'

'I can take an 'int.'

Owen knew what Gladdy would say about his article. It lacked a 'cutting edge.' This was what he was always asking for, 'cutting edges', but it did not come naturally to Owen to be aggressive and controversial. 'Hit them on the nose,' was another expression Gladdy used. 'Readers like things in black and white.' He wanted a piece that would get the readers' backs up. To be fair Gladdy had never spiked one of Owen's articles but he might. 'Make it more personal. Think of someone you know. O.K. if you don't want to attack anybody, at least think of somebody you want to make an impression on.'

From the Archbishop of Canterbury down there was no lack of opponents in the church. Among those he knew personally was the Bishop of Cirencester, old Frank Malpas, but Frank was such a wet Owen did not feel he was worth taking on. It had to be someone tough who would be capable of understanding the point Owen was making and yet able to counter in a way that made sense. Ideally, it should be a man Owen knew personally. A man? Why not a woman? He suddenly thought of Eleanor.

Eleanor had never married. She had been a singularly successful head of a number of schools, was a fan of Mrs Thatcher and thought she was the equal, if not the superior, of any man. Doubtless she was entirely in favour of the ordination of women. He might write the article with Eleanor in mind but he would not necessarily show it to her.

He woke one morning to find a thaw had set in and the tongue of snow outside was dripping like a squeezed sponge. It was so foggy he could scarcely make out the houses opposite so this was another reason why Eleanor could not drive in from the country. She would not drive after dark and she would not drive in fog; her eyes did not permit it and she begrudged the cost of a taxi. Owen told her not to worry; he was getting on fine. The doctor had been in and told him his blood pressure was down and the urine testing he had been instructed to carry out showed negative every time so there was no excess of sugar in the system. Mrs Springer had been able to cash a cheque for him and the police had called. No development. The young constable had not said so but plainly he was not going to waste time looking for this Mickey Mouse girl.

'Have you made a will, Owen? No! That is really rather irresponsible of you. Just think of the worry and the work it would cause me if you pre-deceased me as no doubt you will. If you died intestate Margaret would take everything. You realise that, I suppose. You are still married under English law. And there's Charlotte who would have a claim in any case if her mother was dead. It isn't for me to say who you should make your will in favour of. Who else is there but me though? I don't say that acquisitively but unless there is a will and it is specific about the beneficiary there is no knowing where the estate would land up. You wouldn't like the thought of Margaret's fella benefiting.'

It was enough to make him wonder whether Eleanor was after all a suitable person to have in mind when writing his article. But he persisted. With no intention of

31

buttering Eleanor up he thought about her carefully and found it more important than ever to emphasise the spiritual qualities of women. What they lost in the ecclesiastical hierarchy, not being priests, they more than made up for in soul. From the earliest times the church had emphasised the sanctity of women. The supreme example was the Virgin Mary herself who owed none of her ascendancy to any priestly function. She was the ultimate embodiment of all the female virtues for she was the great intercessor and harmoniser who radiated love and brought joy.

This might not please Gladdy but it was important to write what he, Owen, believed. Now that he had made up his mind the words came more easily, almost as though there had been a link between the stiffness of manner in his first draft and the blizzard. Now the thaw had come the words flowed as the snow melted and could be heard gurgling out of the downpipes. The snow slipped and slithered from roofs. Nature was no longer frozen and static; it moved, had life. He was in harmony with what was happening outside. Soon the sap would be rising in the Salix Babylonica, crocuses would shine in the square, the days would lengthen and the sun come back. The fog was already lifting and thinning. The sun was indeed coming through and he was coming through too, he was recovering from his attack, he bore no ill will towards the young woman in the Mickey Mouse sweater, he bore no ill will to anyone really, he just wrote and wrote enthusiastically. Not since briefly, as a young man, he had written love poems to Margaret did he feel so inspired.

He showed the article to no one before sending it off to Gladdy. Belatedly he realised that the reader he had in mind was not Eleanor but the Margaret he had once known, not the woman she became but the pretty undergraduate reading mathematics who nevertheless came to his lectures on Roman history. A lot of other non-classics students did too. He was a popular lecturer. And Margaret was following an interest aroused by holiday working on an archaeological dig at Verulamium. She was always so precise in the questions she asked and precise in the way she made a note of his answers. He remembered, too, her pointed nose. After she took her degree they lost touch but she came back again and they went for bicycle rides. For her everything was such fun and that was why his article turned out to be not so very solemn after all.

Eleanor came over when she could drive through the slush. She was a chunky woman with straight grey hair, wearing cavalry twill trousers tucked into brown boots that laced up nearly to her knees. Like the girl robber she wore a woollen jumper but Eleanor's had a palm tree on it because she had bought it on a holiday in Florida. So even Eleanor had her dreams and carried this exotic emblem on her front to reveal as much.

'It is important for you to get exercise, Owen. We'll take a walk. I want to do some shopping anyway.'

'I've had my walk.'

Eleanor looked at him severely. 'I saw your piece in *The Courier*.'

Normally she read the *Telegraph* so this was surprising. 'I wasn't really satisfied with it but the *Courier* chap must have thought it passed muster.'

'Frankly, Owen, I thought it was a bit eccentric.' She must have read the article attentively because as she moved about the room, straightening pictures and banging books together to rid them of dust, she made comments on details. The article was not properly focussed. It purported to be about the female psyche but that was a subject that deserved handling with more detachment. He had let his emotions run away with him and she could not see what there was to get emotional about, anyway not in an article that touched on important questions of theology. Her boots squeaked and she had taken to snorting over the undusted furniture. 'But you were always a dreamer.'

'Nothing wrong with that.'

'There is when you extend your dreaming to the point of fantasy.'

It was almost as though she knew about his dream. Had Arthur Minchin told her in spite of being told not to? Owen would not ask. 'You're making me cross, Eleanor.'

She took time to consider this rebellious remark. 'There's something about you.' She looked him straight in the eye in that intimidating way of hers that must have quelled the exuberance of numberless schoolgirls. 'It's a bit late to have to face up to it. In life there are winners and losers.' It was her end of term tone of voice. 'I suppose some people would say I was one of the winners. But you? Well, a loser, I suppose.'

He did not feel a loser. He told her he wished she would leave him alone and this only made her scornful. 'And I wish you would give up this journalism and get on with your real work. You've been talking for years about your notes on Cicero. What have you to show for them? You ought to have had a paper in some learned journal years ago. You're a sick man, Owen, and you may not have much time left.'

No, he was certainly not a loser and Eleanor's claim to be a winner was vulgar. The state the world was in – wars, massacres, famines – how could anybody in their privileged position be anything but humbly grateful? For God's sake! They knew where their next meal was coming from. Even in this foul weather they were warm and dry. And Eleanor counted herself successful just because she'd had good jobs in which she had enjoyed ordering people about and seen her name in the Honours List by way of reward. When she said he was a loser he knew she had his failed marriage in mind, that and his failure to be appointed Dean. What, in the ultimate scale of things, did these so-called failures amount to? In his non-prayers he had been given reassurances. He was not alone. Wherever he went – and it was the passing from the snow garden to the heated plant house that came to mind – he was accompanied by a loving presence and his main sorrow was that the love he returned was so feeble in comparison. If he had been a woman it would have been stronger. Wasn't that, after all, what lay behind his thinking on the ordination of women?

'It's your birthday next week, Eleanor. I'd like to take you out to lunch.'

'Whatever for?' For years they had observed a pact never to send each other Christmas cards or give birthday presents.

'We could go to the Randolph.'

'Out of the question. You're not well enough. In any case there's your diabetes which I don't suppose they'd cater for. Besides, I wouldn't like it. It's not the way we behave.'

'I insist.'

Eleanor showed her amazement. 'As a matter of fact I've got Molly Prince staying with me and I was going to invite Betty Folkes. Just the three of us. A nice little do.' They were old chums of Eleanor's, hard-bitten old school-marms like herself.

'You could bring them too. It would be a real birthday lunch.'

He could see she was tempted. 'It's nice of you, Owen, but it would be a bad precedent. Start going in for entertainments like this and there's no knowing where it might end.'

This was so absurd it made him quite merry. 'You mean you might have to give me lunch on my birthday too. Not at all. I promise.'

'I'll think about it. But I have to tell you it seems unlikely. You know Molly and Betty. They'd have nothing to wear. Neither would I for that matter.'

'Then come here and Mrs Springer can grill some salmon steaks. And we'll drink champagne.'

The more Eleanor resisted the more enthusiastic Owen became. He had never seen her so much on the defensive. Love drove him on, love not only for Eleanor but for that strange couple, Molly and Betty. He saw himself waiting on them in the modest setting of his flat. But the Randolph was where he really wanted to take them.

'You're not yourself, Owen. Must be the pills. I wonder whether you know what you are really doing.'

No, he didn't. Or saying. Or thinking. There were many corners of his mind where these uncertainties arose. The love of God did indeed pass all understanding; so much was it beyond his understanding the very thought of it must surely stand for some profounder truth. His whole life and what had given meaning to his life – scholarship, teaching, love for Margaret, even the green parasol for his mother's birthday – were just symbols. Everything offered as an explanation of life was couched in language that seemed, and only seemed, to refer to reality – love, sacrifice, redemption – but in fact these words had no literal meaning. They stood for something else. What? Behind the words he had enough faith, thank God, to believe there was a reality even he, feeble as he was, could touch.

Eleanor threw her shoulders back and struck her be-brave let's-face-it attitude. 'I'll think it over. I'll talk to Molly and Betty. Perhaps it would be simpler if you came and joined us at my house.'

That would not be the same. No getting a straight answer from Eleanor there and then. She would telephone. To him, deep down, it did not really matter what she decided, in spite of what he had said. Issuing the invitation was what really mattered and he could see by Eleanor's puzzled frown that the gesture had been worthwhile. It might be possible to reach even her and find she could be fitted into his dream.

2
Charlotte

He loved giving parties and going to the opera which was bad luck for Charlotte who cared for neither. Before they were married the magic of just being with him was enough to carry her through evenings at the Met and so successfully that Daniel thought she might not be as besotted with Verdi, Wagner, Strauss and the rest as he was but she really appreciated it all deep down. He thought she was one of those music lovers who went for Bach and Beethoven but thought opera just a bit vulgar. The truth was that Charlotte was not a music lover at all, unless you counted pop and jazz as music which Daniel plainly did not. When he had his posting to London she realised there would be no escaping from opera there but thought there would be fewer parties.

Not a bit of it. Daniel took a long time settling on the right apartment. That was because he wanted at least one really large room where they could entertain and it was a couple of months before they found what he was looking for, off Kensington Church Street. It was a smaller version of the service apartment they had in East 72nd Street, complete with what they called a porter in London who sat at a desk in the hall and phoned up before admitting visitors.

'Not ideal, but it will do. It will have to do.' Daniel had paced out the main sitting room and said they could get up to thirty guests in there and still have room for a buffet and drinks table. 'The bartenders can stand with their backs to that open door and we'll have a girl going round with a tray.'

Charlotte's idea of a social evening was a small dinner party where they could all sit and have a general conversation. These big parties where everybody stood with glasses in their hands and roared at each other confused and exhausted her, particularly now she was pregnant.

'We've got to get to know people, honey,' was what Daniel said when she tried to discourage him. 'It's not only the Wheatley people. There are men in one or two other firms I want to soften up. In this game you've got to get in the right network and that's not done in the City. You've got to bring the wives into the network and you can only do that with socialising.'

The Wheatley Fund Managers were pooling resources with the Minotaur Group of New York – at least that is the way the Wheatley Fund put it but in fact they were being taken over and Daniel, as a Minotaur man, was there in London to see the operation stayed sweet. The bottom line was recommending which of the Wheatley board should be kept on and which should be eased out.

Charlotte knew more than most business wives did about this kind of transaction because she was a lawyer who had specialised in company law. She did particularly well at law school but even so the job she got at the

Gurnas and Dark law firm in Baltimore was very junior, not much better than supervising the mail. But within two years she had a desk of her own and a couple of years later became a junior partner. From this point on it was company law that took up most of her time. She really worked at it, began to be so well thought of in Gurnas and Dark that she was, under Dick Butler a senior partner, put on to the Minotaur assignment. Minotaur had, of course, their own lawyers so Dick Butler and she were mainly concerned with work Minotaur farmed out to them. They were always in and out of the Minotaur offices and this is how Charlotte met Daniel Dancer Blair who was quite a bit older than her but full of fun.

Daniel continued to be full of fun, even after they were married and Charlotte found it just marvellous to be with him. He was a burly man with broad shoulders who had, he said, been quite a footballer in his younger days, not in the professional class but good enough to get an outing with one of the top amateur teams who turned out on Sundays in one of the parks. He grew a lot of dark brown hair and had it tightly sculpted so wore it like a helmet. He seemed to be charged with so much energy Charlotte said he was capable of giving little electric shocks when touched; that was not true but it conveyed something of his dynamism. Yet he spoke quietly and slowly, undoubtedly Ivy League, his eyes big and brown, intent unblinkingly on whoever he was talking to.

Charlotte was a career woman. She was not going just to be Mrs Blair. Daniel warmly approved her decision to carry on working after their marriage; it simply meant he hired a housekeeper, Mrs Dwight, who ran the East 72nd Street apartment for them and stayed on there while they were in Europe. So the place was always ready and waiting when, as Daniel expected, they would be making their frequent return trips. He loved buying flowers. Normally the buying of flowers was left to her but Daniel liked to drop into the florist's himself and come home with bunches of sweet-smelling freesias with maidenhair fern, daffodils and tulips in the season, then roses. He said she must always have flowers about her, because with her clear, pre-Raphaelite skin (that is how he put it) she was as fresh as Aphrodite, newly sprung from the foam of the sea to be goddess of gardens and flowers.

So against this attentiveness and the uninhibited ardour of his love-making she reckoned opera and noisy parties counted for little. Charlotte worked at both, though. He gave her Kobbé's big opera encyclopedia and she read up each opera before they went to the performance. *Aida* was not too bad because the production was so spectacular and even she could pick out the tunes in *Carmen*. But, for her, there were longueurs in both which induced irrelevant thoughts; Carmen was too fat and did not look much of a temptress. Baron Ochs in *Rosenkavalier*, on the other hand, was too weedy. From time to time fresh air came puffing out from the stage as though someone in the background had opened a window on to the street; and she could smell the scenery, she could actually smell the paint – her sense of smell had always been acute – and it sickened her. The really low point came in Strauss's *Ariadne auf Naxos*. Low point is perhaps an inadequate way to express what happened; it was more of a crisis.

Charlotte had not felt particularly well that evening and wondered whether she could make that an excuse for not going. Daniel was always so boisterously well himself he never took other people's ailments at all seriously, not even Charlotte's when she suggested he took somebody else for a change. Out of the question. The production was dark and Ariadne seemed to spend a lot of time just sitting on a little platform bemoaning her lot at great length and in German. Charlotte knew the singer was Swedish which made matters worse because she once had, and she had almost forgotten it, an unfortunate experience with a Swedish diplomat in Washington, and was prejudiced against all Scandinavians as a result. (At a reception he had pulled her behind a palm tree and tried to put a big, hairy-backed hand, down the front of her dress.) Ariadne was going on excessively and Charlotte rebelled.

'I'm sorry, Daniel,' she said. 'I can't take any more. I'm going home.'

'But this is one of the great Ariadnes. It's like Callas's Medea. And Zerbinetta is enchanting. You can't miss this.'

'You stay. Just get me a cab.'

They were at the end of the row and could get out. So that is what they did, Daniel returned to his seat and she went back to the apartment alone to take a bath and lie on the bed in her nightdress to await his homecoming. He did not even ask how she felt but enthused about the production until she started to groan in misery. The very next day she called in a doctor who looked carefully into her eyes and said she was probably pregnant but he'd have to do a test before being sure. Yes, it turned out she was pregnant and Charlotte's realisation of the fact came not when the doctor told her but when she heard Ariadne's despair in the half-light.

So Kobbé was not one of the books she packed for London but this did not mean she gave up accompanying Daniel to the opera. It just meant she gave up playing the game according to his rules and was just her own philistine self and getting as much fun as she could out of operatic absurdities. They went to Glyndebourne where Falstaff nearly sat on a chair that was not there. And there was a blissful moment at Covent Garden when Tosca tripped over Scarpia's corpse. But these diversions were all too rare. Daniel did not seem to notice her fortitude or, if he did, appeared not to care. Nothing was to interfere with his pleasure. What struck Charlotte about these operatic excursions was the number of people he knew and could talk to familiarly during the intervals. He had been coming to England for years, cultivating friends and acquaintances so perhaps it was not altogether surprising. Even so, it was a bit of a paradox that she, who had been born in England, and spent the first few years of her life there should feel less at home in London than he, a native-born American, did.

In the Crush Bar at Covent Garden he was hailed noisily by a man who opened his mouth wide and leaned away as though to emphasise the mock-awe with which Daniel's presence struck him. It was quite a dramatic performance. It might have been the Bird-Catcher starting back at his unexpected encounter with the Wicked Moor in the very opera, *The Magic Flute*, they were attending. 'My dear Daniel. I must buy you champagne. This is an occasion for celebration. I must buy you lots of champagne. Zoe.' He turned to the woman who accompied him. 'Darling. You remember Dan Blair. The last man to give a party at the top of the Post Office Tower. It proved too much for the fabric. Ever afterwards it had to be closed to the public.'

Charlotte was introduced. He was Edgar Flook, a big name in television (Daniel said) and his wife Zoë. They both reproached Daniel for not having warned them he was in town and then turned on Charlotte with a blaze of enthusiasm and more talk – they did not bother to take it in turns – than she felt able to cope with. Flook was wearing a scarlet cummerbund and his wife carried a black cloak lined with silk of not quite the same colour. Flook began talking about Mozart and Freemasonry, saying the opera was one that almost made him want to be a Freemason but he was always put off by the thought of the way they dressed up in funny clothes. He said, with a great wink and a thumb jerked in the direction of his cummerbund, that he was never a man for sartorial ostentation. The bell rang that brought the interval to a close but not before the Blairs had been invited to dinner the following Thursday fortnight. And so it went on. Encounters, merry times recalled, invitations. This was not the England Charlotte remembered.

She could remember her father, just about, not as a father but as a man who had a bicycle that ticked like a watch as he wheeled it out through the front gate in the sunshine. He wore a dark hat with a wide brim, had a shiny red face and an adam's apple that stuck out over a white band. This man in bicycle clips, one foot on a pedal as he pushed off, the other leg high in the air as he moved away, was the same who took her and her mother on the river. There was such a stretch of water she could see clouds reflected in it and hear singing that came from a white, chalet-like building on the bank. He stood up, pushing the punt with a pole past shining green trees. That was about all she remembered of England and, to be honest, she was not entirely sure she did remember it. The bicycle, yes, she remembered that and the way it ticked but the clouds in the water and the green grass might have come out of photographs of her as a child. Picnic photographs, her mother said. They often went on picnics but she never mentioned the father and Charlotte did not ask about him. She was interested only in the present and that was full of happenings; a red tricycle, a huge green plastic crocodile she could ride on in the pool, and a boy who splashed her. Later on, school and lots of friends. Anyway, she had a new father and loved him very much.

One of the first parties Daniel and she were invited to was given by an Indonesian diplomat at his home some-where up a hill in North London. They ate delicious food and listened to tapes of gamelan music which Charlotte rather enjoyed; then she was whisked away by her host and introduced to a painter, Fulke Marshal, who had recently come from working in Bali. Charlotte had heard of Marshal who told her the Museum of Modern Art had just bought one of his paintings. He was a quietly spoken man with a shy smile Charlotte rather took to. The surprise, though, was that he knew Daniel. They had met on one of Daniel's earlier London trips.

He came over. 'I see you've found Fulke, dear. He's probably the greatest painter since – well, who shall we say? What was the name of that water lilies man? Yes, Monet. Isn't it about time you had a great retrospective? The world is waiting for it. Come on Fulke, no mock modesty. You're a great man and it is a privilege to be in the same room with you.'

'I'm just amazed at the number of people you know, Daniel.' The famous painter had been taken over by a bearded man who spoke to him in French. Daniel shrugged. 'As a matter of fact there's a friend I'd very much like you to meet.'

Charlotte was sure it was a woman. 'Is she here?'

'Oh no. It's a meeting that will have to be arranged.'

'Is it an old flame?'

He chuckled. 'Aha! We'll have to see, won't we?'

A company car complete with uniformed driver was waiting to take them home because one of the first battles Daniel had won at Wheatley's was for just such a perk.

He said it was the least the directors owed themselves, particularly at a time when they were transferring so much head office work out into the country, to Milton Keynes. They would need to pop down there at a moment's notice. For this a properly staffed car pool was a necessity. And directors should be able to call on it for just such functions as this do at the Indonesian diplomat's house. Also trips to Glyndebourne, to West End theatres and, for Charlotte's benefit, to her ante-natal clinic in Harley Street. Parking problems being what they were how else would you get about? So Len, in his blue uniform and peaked cap with the Wheatley badge at the front, who had been waiting for a good three hours, picked them up.

'You're very quiet,' Daniel said as they glided down Highgate Hill. 'What are you thinking about?'

'Nothing particularly. I'm just a little tired.' She had, as a matter of fact, been thinking about the old friend Daniel was planning to introduce her to. She built up quite a picture of the woman. She'd be a great opera fan, that went without saying, probably had long blonde hair done up in some natty way, and wore pricey clothes. Charlotte wouldn't be surprised if she was an expert on wine too. For Daniel to want her to meet up with his wife indicated something else too. But what? Made her sound harmless. Perhaps she owned a Wimbledon debenture – Daniel was a tennis fan too – and that would give them easy access to the lawn tennis championships when they came round. Charlotte loved Daniel dearly but she well knew he was vain and a bit thick-skinned so it was quite possible he wanted to show off this woman as an early conquest and there was no calculation of any other advantage. That didn't ring entirely true. She was probably a luscious and bejewelled opera-loving houri now safely married to a man who owned an ocean-going yacht and loved taking his friends on Mediterranean cruises. Added to which this houri had just become a grandmother. When Daniel asked her what she was thinking about she naturally could not answer truthfully. It would have sounded as though she thought what a mean bastard he was and that would not be true at all.

Daniel's love making was as vigorous and uninhibited as ever. Charlotte had asked about this at the ante-natal clinic and told it was in order during early pregnancy but she ought to ask again, say three or four months before her confinement was due. Charlotte was beginning to think of herself not as one person but two. Would to God the relationship between all three of them, and any other child she would have, remained as close and as loving.

She wrote to Meg from time to time to tell her about the glitzy life she and Daniel were leading and, on one occasion, to suggest Meg and Simon might come and stay for a while. She had never called her mother anything but Meg or her step-father anything but Simon. *Shime* to begin with when she could not get her tongue round the word. They were now living down in Florida, on the Gulf Coast, where Simon still taught part time at Tampa but put most of his energy into writing Sci-Fi with modest success. Meg's replies became so perfunctory that Charlotte took to telephoning.

'Sweet of you to ask us,' said Meg, 'but by the sound of the fun you're having we'd only get in the way.'

'We'd just love to have you.'

'The truth is, Charlotte, the thought of England is a bit depressing. Long grey afternoons with the wind howling in the chimney.'

'You know it isn't a bit like that. We're having the sunniest weather.'

Meg had always been reluctant to visit her native

country even when her parents were still alive. The European holidays they took were usually in Italy, Greece or Austria where Simon had cousins. Meg would have returned for her father's funeral but there was some mystery about what then happened. An air-line ticket was bought and clothes hurriedly stuffed into a suitcase only for the trip to be cancelled at the last minute. Judging by the way she shut herself away for a time only to emerge not exactly tearful but certainly a bit morose she really wanted to attend her father's funeral. But something stopped her. Other proposed trips to England were aborted by her own decision. They were to have flown from Salzburg to Heathrow so that Simon could visit the Cavendish Laboratory at Cambridge, where he had never been, so that he could work it into one of his stories. Once again Meg did not make the trip. Simon went alone, she and Charlotte flew via Frankfurt back to the States. England was not completely out of bounds. Meg took Charlotte to meet her grandmother in Leicester. The old lady frightened Charlotte by her manner which was grim and when the news came through some months later that she had died Charlotte's first thought was that she would not have to meet her again. That was a funeral Meg did attend. Meg was the only child and beneficiary of her mother's will. She sold everything, house, furniture, books, and the money was used to buy this place down in Florida long before they had any thought of moving there for good.

'Well, how are you feeling, anyway?'

Charlotte reported on her latest trip to the ante-natal clinic. 'But you know how it is,' she said. 'Physically O.K. Everything is fine. I just find it very strange to be carrying another human being. I'm two people.'

'It comes to us all.'

'I just *feel* so responsible. You know?'

'No, I don't really. I can't remember thinking that.'

'It just gives me this feeling of – well, how can I put it? Otherness. Here I am. I'm not just me.'

'You're just living it up too much.'

'If you came over we could have a real talk.'

'It would do you much more good to come over here and sit by the pool. We were out in the dinghy and saw flying fish. Fantastic. Quite a rarity in these parts but there they were hopping like outsize fleas.'

Charlotte was sure Meg's reluctance to come to England stemmed from the failure of her first marriage which, now that she was pregnant, Charlotte thought about more and more. She thought of her father who, if genetics meant anything at all, would have some part in the child she was to bear. Meg never talked of him except on one rare occasion when she said he was more interested in books than he was in her, though once he had threatened her with violence which seemed to show he had non-academic interests too. Something told Charlotte she was lying and the thought must have shown on her face because Meg became angry and said, 'I regret nothing in my life. Nothing. Don't you ever forget that.' Thereafter the subject was taboo.

Charlotte knew her father was a lot older than her mother. That made him what? Seventy. As much as that perhaps. Probably he had married again. Possibly he was dead. It was unnatural that she was to bear the grandchild of a man of whom she was so ignorant and for the first time she thought of finding out what had happened to him. She mentioned it to Daniel.

'Why not?' he said. 'Shouldn't be too difficult.'

'Meg wouldn't be pleased.'

Daniel shrugged. He had Wheatley problems so it was

understandable he was not terribly interested. They had all to do with the relative emphasis the firm was putting on different markets, bonds, futures, even currency speculation which was dear to Daniel's heart unlike the rest of the Wheatley board who seemed to think there was something unpatriotic in deals that anticipated a fall in sterling. Either work was the preoccupation or he was thinking of that opera-loving houri of his whom Charlotte was still waiting to meet.

When the weather was good Charlotte went walking in Kensington Gardens and never failed to be struck by the expanse of the place and the way, just by sitting on a bench and looking west, there was so much sky to look at. In the American parks she knew the tall buildings all round nibbled at the sky but here most of the buildings were low and there were whole cloudscapes to look at, sometimes with a marine brightness over there beyond the palace and the embassies that hinted there was a great harbour with yachts only just hidden and further out would be the ocean itself.

When she told Meg that she was not alone, that someone else was with her, the words had just popped out without any great thought on her part. But here, sitting in the park, she felt she had uttered some truth unwittingly and the other person was not her unborn child. Or, rather, that the 'other' was the unborn child but some thing or some one was speaking to her through the child. Well, pregnant women have strange ideas. This one was pleasant, even comforting.

One hot afternoon she was walking back from the Gardens when she must have lost her way because she found herself in an unfamiliar narrow street. Here was a church with its main door wide open to show darkness and a glimmer of light within. Feeling tired, she thought she would go in and rest. She found herself in a church where lit candles fluttered in front of a screen so assumed it must be Roman Catholic. She seemed to be alone but there was no knowing who might be hidden in those shadows. Then she saw that on the screen above the candles was an ikon of the Virgin Mary such as she had seen on holidays in Greece and realised she was in an Orthodox church.

She was not religious but she was not the atheist that Simon declared himself to be. Meg used to take her to the Episcopalian church at Easter and Christmas but it meant little to her. Even as a child, more so as a young woman, she was too sure of herself and felt no need of supernatural support even if she could have been brought to believe what Christians were supposed to believe. She declined confirmation and Meg did not insist though it was an unspoken thought between them that it might have been expected of the daughter of an ordained minister. Before going to Law School her church going was for social reasons. Her friends went, there was a tennis club and a lot of dating went on. Even that stopped when she went to college. Daniel's background was Baptist but that meant nothing either. Their wedding was the usual civil affair with a reception in the mayor's parlour afterwards and she would not have wished it otherwise.

A small candle cost five pence, a large one ten. She slipped a coin into the box, chose one of the larger candles and lit it, taking some care to fix it carefully in a holder. To show respect. That is what they had said on those Greek holidays. Even Simon had lit a candle. The flickering of the candles caused the ikon to quiver as though with life and Charlotte looked at the long, sombre face for some time though the fumes from the candles made her want to sneeze and she had to restrain herself for fear of blowing some of them out. In the fresh air she carried the reek of candle fat and stale incense with her but she did not mind. In fact she felt quite pleased with herself.

Back at the apartment block the porter said a man was waiting to see her. In fact he had been waiting for half an hour.

'He says he's from Findlay Caterers and wanted me to let him go up but I couldn't do that, ma'am.'

'My God! The party!' She had completely forgotten. The man from Findlay Caterers came forward, saying he was a bit worried because he had the van parked outside on double yellow lines.

'Is it O.K. for us to bring the stuff up? My mate is sitting in the van.'

'Sure! I'll go up and let you in. I'm so sorry you've been held up.'

That was the not very propitious start to their very first party in the Blair home and once she had let the caterers in with their trestles, their glasses, their bottles of drink and told them how she wanted things arranged her main thought was whether there was time to have her hair done. For God's sake! What was the matter with her? Her hair was frightful and she probably stank of that church. Fortunately it was still early enough to make up for lost time. She telephoned the Harrod's hairdressing department and they made no difficulty at all.

The party was a success. Even Daniel was pleased. By 6 p.m. the first arrivals were a couple of Wheatley men with their wives. Then came the Cultural Attaché from the American Embassy unaccompanied, a couple from the *Financial Times*, the London editor with wife of the *Wall Street Journal*, various city editors, opera people, the manager of London Ballet and wife – Charlotte knew them all by name because she and Daniel had checked the guest list together but she knew none of them by sight and Daniel had to do the introductions. The Flooks were the exception. At Daniel's request nobody had dressed up but the Flooks were in full fig, she in an apricot gown of some splendour and he in white tie with tails, medals and what Charlotte took to be the badge of some order round his neck. After the party they were going on to the Royal Academy dinner and Flook apologised if anyone thought they were overdressed but time pressed, you know! He abstemiously drank tomato juice not so very much darker in colour than his own face, no doubt with the wines at the coming dinner in mind. For no obvious reason he was shaking with laughter and already into a story about the amateur theatricals that went on in the village where the Flooks had a retreat. Against his advice they had taken on *Macbeth*. Anyway, a rather simple-minded religious sort of chap had been cast as Duncan and he could not bring himself to utter the line, 'What bloody man is that?' because in his dictionary the word bloody was a swear word. He was assured that in this context it was not, so Duncan steeled himself to bring out the, to him, foul word. At the crucial moment Duncan hesitated and then said fiercely, 'What bugger is that?' Yells of laughter. Yes, it was funny. The Brits laughed because the word was still rude in England but the American Cultural Attaché looked mystified.

'I want you to meet an old friend of mine,' Daniel said to Charlotte and a sinewy-looking woman with coppery tinted fair hair bounced up, raising her eyes towards the ceiling in a way that was plainly meant to be fetching. 'When I first knew Cyrilly she was in the Covent Garden chorus, Cyrilly Joris. But she is now Cyrilly Clarke-Moodie. Or should I say Lady Clarke-Moodie?'

Charlotte was sure this was the houri. Judging by her clothes she was rich but there was no knowing whether

her husband had that ocean-going yacht; there was nothing nautical about her but then at a party like this why should there be? It fitted that she had been in the opera chorus. Charlotte greeted Daniel's ex-mistress coolly and checked herself from remarking she was glad the lady had come well enough out of the affair to marry money and into a title.

'My husband and I are hoping to tempt you and Daniel down to Goodwood.'

So that was it. Racing. Lady Clarke-Moodie was about fifty which put her older than Daniel which made it likely that he had cast her off rather than the other way round. No hard feelings, apparently. Daniel was not even afraid the lady might be indiscreet for he made off to talk to the *Financial Times* man and she was able to say confidentially to Charlotte, 'He doesn't change. Always bubbling. Why he's so popular, of course. Well, what a lovely wife he's found for himself at last. He is very, very lucky, my dear. Luckier than he deserves, perhaps.'

It was nine o'clock before the last guests departed and Daniel, having enjoyed himself hugely, stayed high. In mock-exhaustion he sprawled in a chair, his jacket undone and his shirt rucked up showing a bit of bare belly. Charlotte supervised as the hired barman and waitress collected the glasses, bottles, the uneaten asparagus rolls and canapés. They packed all this stuff away in hampers and then they were gone.

'I suppose that Lady Whatever was the person you were wanting me to meet.' Charlotte was finishing off a tray of cocktail sausages.

'Come again.'

'The old flame.'

'Cyrilly? Jeez no! Did I say an old flame? No, a friend. Anyway, it's not female. It's male.'

'Well, who is he?'

Daniel sat there grinning like a man with a delicious secret to reveal and Charlotte found this good-humoured smirking even more unsettling when she understood what the secret was.

'A boy. No, not a boy. He's a young man called Tomas Rais.' He spelled the names out so that there was no mistaking it for Thomas Rice. 'He's Czech. And there's a strong probability he's my son.'

'Your son?' Charlotte's legal training helped her to cushion the shock. This was not company law but she had learned how to deal with unwelcome surprises. Part of the training had been to ride them. Never get caught out, Dick Butler of Gurnas and Dark used to say, or if you are don't show it. 'Tell me more.'

'You know I was a Rhodes scholar.'

'What's that?'

'I told you about this year I had at Oxford. A Rhodes Scholar is American or German or from the Common-wealth. He gets financed out of some trust. So I had an award and studied public administration for a year. I was just twenty-one. I used to go to parties at the American Embassy here. The Cultural Attaché had been a Rhodes scholar too. I met this woman from the Czech Embassy there and we had one of those affairs. Her name was Vera. At the time I just thought I was being recruited. No way could I be recruited.'

'What do you mean, recruited?'

'As an agent. I just played along for the fun of it, then one day I phoned the Czech Embassy. I was passed from one apparatchik to another apparatchik. I just wanted to speak to Vera. How naive can you get! I was told she'd gone back to Prague. The Iron Curtain was still up in those days. The Cold War was on. No word from her and of course it was impossible for me to contact her.' After a pause. 'Even if I wanted to.'

'So they weren't trying to recruit you.'

Daniel was still grinning but not so broadly, recognising perhaps there was a serious side to what he was saying. But the important thing was to be robust and goodhumoured.

'No they were not trying to recruit me. Sharp of you to see that. I didn't at the time. I knew a guy in the CIA and later on I asked him and that's what he came up with, they weren't trying to recruit me but he didn't rule out a bit of blackmail. No chance. So it fizzled out.'

'What about this probable son?'

'I couldn't even have remembered what she looked like but a while ago this letter from Prague came and it was from Vera. She said she'd had my son all those years ago and now he was in England. He'd come to London with a Prague theatre group and walked out on them. They were hosted at the Old Yard Theatre. The Czechs are still tough on their dissidents though things must be a bit different these days. They must be different because she felt free to write.'

'How did she know what address to write to?'

'She remembered my college and wrote there. They update the addresses of all their alumni.'

'So you met him?'

'Sure I met him. He's a nice guy. But do you know what? He doesn't want anything to do with me. He was quite mad at his mother for writing.'

'Is this all you've got to go on?'

'Whether he's my son or not? Yeah! It's only Vera's say-so. There are blood tests but the way this kid is he'd just go berserk at the idea. It isn't that he rejects this story he's my son. He doesn't care. He doesn't care whose son he is. He looks like he might be my son though.'

'You still want to fix this meeting?'

'He works as a trainee stage manager at the Old Yard Theatre and you can just walk into that place. They have a lunch buffet for the staff and anybody can walk in and buy a bowl of soup and bread and cheese. That's how I've met him.'

'Why didn't you tell me all this before?'

'Charlotte, you're right. I should have done exactly that. First of all I thought I was being conned. I still may be. But I changed my mind when I knew what Tomas's attitude was. He's always refused to meet me away from the theatre but I'll get him here. That I will do.'

Charlotte made it her business to find out more about the Old Yard Theatre. The Cultural Affairs Attaché, whose name was Charles Duffy, told her it was a small subsidised theatre near King's Cross. 'Government money through the Arts Council,' he said, 'but that doesn't stop them from biting the hand that feeds them. They're anti-establishment and how! I'd say they were left wing but I guess they'd say they were just radical. If you know anyone who works there they'd be wacky. Sort of way out. No more than some off-Broadway outfits I guess. They do classics in a quirky sort of way but most of their stuff is new. Would you like tickets? Let me see, what are they doing now? It's a piece called *Battler's Price*. About the drug scene.'

No, Charlotte did not want tickets but she remembered what Daniel said about their buffet food and took a cab there one lunch time. The building looked ancient and not well worn with pilasters stuck on a crumbling facade; the area might have been smart once but now was run down, with the ground floors of Victorian dwellings turned into shops and even ateliers turning out light fittings and cheap furniture. Huge posters trumpeting the current show were on both sides of the entrance where the box office was functioning in the care of a frizzy haired girl who was doing a crossword in one of the papers. But she was very friendly. When Charlotte asked where everyone was eating she just said, 'You press? Up those stairs and follow your nose.'

Charlotte had no shyness about walking into a crowd of people she did not know. They were mostly about her age, young that is to say, but in jeans and trainers, some queueing for food, some standing and eating off a shelf, some just sitting on the floor to eat so that they had to be stepped over. It was noisy. Charlotte bought herself some moussaka and a glass of red wine before finding room on the shelf; here she was joined by a sharp-eyed man in what looked like jogging gear who said, 'Hallo! Do I know you?' He turned out to be the General Manager, Mike.

'I'm a gatecrasher,' said Charlotte, giving her name.

'That's O.K. but we can't have too many members of the public otherwise there'd not be enough grub to go round. I ought to turn you out really but seeing as you've bought something I'll turn a blind eye. Why the hell didn't you lie and say you were from the Arts Council?'

'I'm really looking for a young man called Tomas Rais. You know him?'

'What do you want him for?'

'It's just a family matter.'

'A bit cool, isn't it, walking in here, eating our food, drinking our wine and asking questions?'

'Sorry. You're right to be upset. To be fair, I've paid for this food.'

'You got it cheap. It's subsidised by the company and

you're not entitled to fatten yourself at our expense. Now, eat up and then I must ask you to leave.'

'But what about Tomas Rais?'

'Out!' His jokey manner was wearing thin. He had probably decided she was a snooper, even an official of some kind, could be the police, and Tomas needed protecting. Charlotte suspected something of this kind and could think of nothing better to do than produce her passport and say, 'Look, Mike, I'm harmless. I'm harmless. I'm an American citizen. What could be more harmless than that?'

Mike shouted with laughter and would have put his arm round her if she had allowed it. The exchanges were attracting attention. A few of the spectators gathered so as not to miss the fun and Mike, seeing he had an audience, said, 'We don't know anybody called Tom Rais here, do we? Of course we don't. This harmless American lady seems to think otherwise but we're not going to allow her to browbeat us, are we?'

He might have been expecting a chorus of, 'Oh no, we won't' or, 'We don't know anybody called Tom Rais,' as in a Christmas pantomime, but at this point a tall young man stepped forward and placed himself in front of Charlotte, saying, 'I am Tomas Rais. What do you want of me?'

She looked at him with interest. He was about eighteen or nineteen, much taller than she was so she had to look up at his face. He seemed amused. He had not shaved for a couple of days, was scruffy in a piratical sort of way, especially as he wore a gold earring. But what chiefly struck her was his hair, it was thick and chestnutty, the colour of Daniel's and she could see that it could be cut more closely to look like Daniel's helmet. Neither his eyes nor the shape of his face reminded her particularly of

Daniel but the hair did and she was sure that this gangling freebooter was indeed Daniel's son.

'I'm Daniel Blair's wife.'

'Oh! It is very flattering for me but I wish you had not come.' His English was excellent if a little formal. 'But it is noisy in here and it would be better if we found somewhere quiet. You understand, Mrs Blair, that the last thing I want to be is discourteous but nevertheless there are certain considerations. Will you come with me?'

She was ushered through a door, down some steps and into the theatre itself where a carpenter was on stage banging away in some part of the set. It represented a bed-sitter with a bed in one corner, a cooking stove in another, tables and chairs as though set up for a discussion group; through a window there was a view of chimneys and tiled roofs so the room was meant to be high up. After placing Charlotte in one of the stalls Tomas went and had a shouted conversation with the carpenter, then returned and said, 'He has promised to be quiet for five minutes.'

Tomas's manner was so courteous, almost deferential, that Charlotte was charmed. 'You have a good accent.'

'I am a mimic. A good ear. And I listened to BBC radio. Did Mr Blair send you?' Tomas took the seat next to hers. They looked straight ahead, speaking quietly because of the curious deadness of an empty theatre.

'He doesn't even know I'm here.'

'Then why have you come? He tried to give me some money and that made me angry. Yes, I know it was silly to be angry. He only meant to be kind but I was angry because – '

She waited. 'You wanted to show your independence?'

61

He shrugged. 'Now you pursue me too, Mrs Blair. Why can't you just leave me alone?'

'Your mother wouldn't be angry would she? After all, she wrote to Daniel.'

'My mother is a fool and her husband is a fool too.'

'She said Daniel was your father. Do you accept that?'

'The question does not interest me, Mrs Blair. I have no wish to be – ' He hesitated for the appropriate word but when it came it was the right one. – 'No wish to be compromised!'

He was very strange, no doubt about that, and she could only guess his strangeness had something to do with what made him leave Czechoslovakia. The communist state had collapsed. There was some of the old freedom there but that was not enough for Tomas apparently. Had he cleared out for more personal reasons? A love affair could have gone wrong. The word 'compromise' was odd though. Did he understand just what it meant? Yes, he did.

'I have to be back at my work. My wish is to be left alone with myself. To be completely independent.'

'No one can be that, Tomas.'

'You are right. People have been kind to me in England but part of me has been angry at that kindness too. I don't want to be – ' another hesitation and the bookish word 'beholden' came out. 'I don't want to be beholden to anyone. The fact that I have been beholden I do not deny. To the authorities. To this theatre. I should be a fool and ungrateful to deny it. But there must come a stop. As this conversation must come to a stop, Mrs Blair. If you will forgive me, I must go.'

He was crazy but touching in his craziness. He was so vulnerable. What had happened to hurt him like this?

Charlotte stood up when he did and he led the way to an exit. On stage the hammering started again.

'It is best if you hear no more of me and I hear no more of Mr Blair.' Then he was gone.

Daniel was called back to New York to consult and he wanted Charlotte to go with him but she said no, she would vegetate a while and catch up on some reading. Daniel's trip meant missing Goodwood with the Clarke-Moodies; she would not go without him, though much pressed. Before Daniel went off she told him about her visit to the Old Yard Theatre and the unsatisfactory talk she had with Tomas.

He grunted. 'I sent him a note, giving this address and telephone number just in case he wakes up and changes his mind. He's just a kid.'

'Did you ever reply to that letter you had from his mother?'

'Sure. But she never wrote back. The way people can get screwed up in Europe these days is past believing. I guess that for some people in Prague the sky had dropped in, Vera being one of them. Working in the Embassy as she did she must have been a hard-liner. For all we know that's the way she brought Tomas up.'

'Did she say whether he knew he was illegitimate?'

'Hell, I wish I could lay hands on that letter. But yes, she said he knew all right and her husband was quite happy he knew and accepted him as though he was his own son.' Daniel seemed to think it was all a bit of a lark. Fathering a bastard was not something to be ashamed of. Just the opposite. He was proud of the macho image it helped to build up and Charlotte guessed he boasted of what he had done to his closer friends like – well, like

63

who? She wondered if the Clarke-Moodies and the Flooks knew. In New York he belonged to the Century Club and she supposed there were one or two guys there who knew all about it. Where did that leave her? It did her no harm. She had no illusions about Daniel but she loved him dearly and would have liked to help in bringing him and Tomas together. Tomas had struck quite a chord with her and it went on reverberating in her memory.

She went to the public library and looked up a few reference books. *Who's Who* had no entry for her father, nor had *Who Was Who* which she consulted in case he was dead. But the latest volume only went up to eight years previous and he could have died since then. But he probably had not rated a *Who's Who* entry anyway. A blank in the *World of Learning*. An obvious move would have been to consult the Oxford telephone directory but there was no certainty, assuming he was alive, that he still lived in that area. Remembering what Daniel said about his college updating information she thought of ringing St Ebbe's (she remembered the name of her father's old college) but somebody in the library there said they did not give information from the college register over the telephone. From time to time during this detective work she thought of Tomas and what he would think. Leave your father alone, he might say. After all this time you can mean nothing to him. He might even find your approach unwelcome and upsetting.

Tomas wanted to cut himself off, for whatever reason, and Daniel thought that was crazy. Charlotte did not think he was crazy; he was a protester and one day they might know why. She could never be like that. She needed people, she needed friends, she needed her mother, she needed Simon, above all she needed Daniel and could not even imagine herself into the isolation Tomas was after. She was sustained by all these people. She was part of a network. How could she live without knowing they were all there? What the hell! The library had all the telephone directories. She pulled down the Oxford directory and found it listed several Barks, one of them being Bark, Rev O., at 11 Lattimore Gardens. Then it occurred to her to look in *Crockford's*. Yes, the same information appeared there with the added letters Rtd. That was her father. No doubt at all. The question was whether to phone or to write. She decided to write.

Some days later there came a beautifully hand-written reply.

My dear child,
You can imagine the amazement with which I read your letter. Yes, I am alive though your tone hinted a doubt. I am enjoying, nay luxuriating in this hot weather, long may it last. You give little news of yourself though that was hardly to be expected in a letter of so exploratory a nature. I gather, however, that you are married and domiciled, albeit temporarily, in London where I never go these days. I long to see you even though I suspect I may well prove a disappointment to you. Recently I learned that I was diabetic. This was a damper – it means I have to go without pudding – but apart from a slight heart trouble I am pretty well. Would you and your husband have time to come and see me? You are thirty years of age by my calculation. I am dizzy at the thought of seeing my dear Char, pronounced Shar, as we called you.

Affectionately
Owen Bark

She telephoned. Two days later she was in Oxford where she was dropped by her cab in front of 11 Lattimore Gardens to find her father waiting on the step.

'The trains from Paddington run every hour so I knew when to expect you. My dear! How beautiful you are!'

He was taller, more gaunt, than she expected and dressed for summer in sandals, light blue slacks and white, open-neck shirt. He looked at her over steel-rimmed half glasses, bright-eyed with delight. 'We have two flights of stairs to climb. No lift. I trust you don't mind that but it doesn't matter if you do because there's nothing I can do about it. The daily climb of these stairs in my exercise. I also walk to the cricket when they are playing in The Parks. I don't suppose you remember me at all.'

'I remember your bicycle.'

One wall of his sitting room, into which he led the way, was taken up with shelves full of books. On his desk was a typewriter with paper in it. So he could have typed the reply to her letter but instead had chosen to write by hand. On a table were two cups and a jar of instant coffee. He was at once busy with getting things from his little kitchen, biscuits, brown sugar, milk. He must have switched on an electric kettle because he came back from the kitchen rubbing his hands and saying, 'It's quite new and switches itself automatically. I hope you had a good journey. People arriving from London these days usually seem worn by their experiences there but you look wonderfully fresh, my dear.'

If he and her mother had stuck together they would not have been living in a flat like this. It was bright and cheerful, with the morning sun flooding in, but Meg was always one for space. She liked big rooms with not a lot of furniture in them and colourful modern paintings, the real thing, original oils not reproductions. Her father was clearly not that way inclined. There were college photographs and an Old Master drawing which she was curious enough to look at more closely. It was a Leonardo, her father said. The original was in Windsor Castle.

'You look like your mother. What news is there of her?'

Charlotte told him. It was incredible this lean stooping man, who was always on the go in spite of his frailty, was her father. She had hoped not so much to see him as to recognise him, not from the one or two photographs her mother had kept, but out of some sense of kinship. Yes, that's him, she had wanted to say. I just feel he's my father and I would have known him if we had met by accident. There was no such recognition.

'Were you married in church, Shar?'

After coffee he reminded her they were in her native city and she probably remembered nothing about it. Would she like to go on a little tour? He phoned for a cab and they drove down St Giles past the Martyrs' Memorial into Broad Street where he pointed out the spot where Latimer and Ridley had in fact been burned; and so on, past colleges and libraries which he identified with precision.

'If you look over there to the right you can get a glimpse of the old city wall.'

They turned into the High and there were more colleges. At the university church he pointed out the statue of the Virgin over the entrance and said she still bore the marks where Cromwell's soldiers had shot at her. Then to St Ebbe's where he dismissed the cab and they walked through the main gate, saluted by the porter, into the Mulberry quad with its single ancient tree and, on its green lawn, a scattering of the fallen purple fruit. This was his world. He had come to Oxford from school and, except for the war years, had spent the rest of his life there. From the eagerness with which he threw information at her it was clear he loved it all. His hold on Oxford and Oxford's hold on him was his compensation for the loss of a wife. She wanted to know whether he had married again but dare not ask. He had written of being dizzy at the thought of seeing her but now that she was with him, walking at his side, she was – well, not dizzy but moved by the realisation he was her father and that she knew so little about him.

They went into the chapel and admired the Grinling Gibbons carving on the reredos. The pulpit with its sounding board was 18th century he said but the place had been pitilessly restored by the Victorians. 'Didn't she just hate that stained glass? At least, it isn't real stained glass. It's some other kind of coloured glass.'

'It's O.K. by me.'

'This is where your mother and I were married. We would have liked you to be baptised here but, as you see, there is no font. No call for one in a college chapel.'

'Where was I christened?'

'In St Margaret's. In the family shawl. I was baptised in it and all the Barks going back to the middle of the last century.'

'What happened to it?'

For this outing Owen had slipped on a dark blue blazer with brass buttons. Here in the chapel he carried the floppy linen hat which he now used to dab his brow. It was a warm day, but not as warm as all that and she wondered whether he was feeling unwell and should be encouraged to go home.

He said he was perfectly all right and was going to take her to lunch to an Italian restaurant. 'What happened to the shawl? That's a point, isn't it? I really don't know. I expect your mother has it.'

'I must ask her. I should like my own child to be christened in it. I'm expecting it in the Fall.'

'Good heavens! What wonderful news. How happy you must be, my dear. And your husband. Just think, that will make me a grandfather.'

'Yes, it is wonderful.'

They went out into the quad. He seemed more moved by her news than seemed entirely sensible and spoke of taking her to see the Master of the College so that he could share the wonderful news. 'He's a new Master. In the post for only five years but a good man. So far as I know he's the first geologist to be the head of a college here. Karl Strauss would love to meet you and rejoice with us. The oldest rock in the world is in Greenland but he went to another part of Greenland and found some that was even older. So they made him a knight and he is now Sir Karl Strauss. But I've just remembered. He was born and brought up in Prague and that is where he is now on a visit, so we can't see him. It's vacation time and there is no one in Oxford. The place is quite deserted.'

That was not how it looked to Charlotte. Out in the town there was so much traffic and so many people Owen hesitated before plunging among them; buses, taxis, trucks, cyclists, shoppers and lots of children, French and German by the sound of them, all milling round in a way he obviously found confusing. She took his arm to help steer him across the street. He had put his hat on and it drooped about his ears. It made him look ancient, like some old peasant, with his long nose and long upper lip which Charlotte now realised she had inherited and, quite possibly, her child would too.

'I've had the most splendid idea.' He had stopped walking. She knew this was to get his breath back but he would not have admitted as much; he pretended this was to show her the site of the inn where Shakespeare had stayed on his journeys between Stratford and London but she could see this was a pretence and that he was really whacked. She wanted to hail a cab.

'Perhaps you're right, my dear.'

Back in his flat she said she often did not eat lunch at all so he was to put that out of his mind. He had a metal-framed tip-up chair which he eased himself into and asked her to manipulate so that his feet were higher than his head. He took a pill and lay with his eyes closed for some time. 'I'm perfectly all right, Shar. I have these little turns and I even welcome the visitor as an old friend. That's how I think of it. The visitor comes upon me. I call her le Fay because she was a Celtic witch, and do you know, Shar, I am half Welsh, you are a quarter Welsh. Your child will be one eighth Welsh. But you see, I am better already. Le Fay has planted her kiss upon my brow and left as quickly as she came.'

'Do you live on your own?'

'A woman comes in. She cleans up and at a pinch cooks a meal. But don't be concerned. I have been so excited at seeing you. To learn that I was to be grandfather was the final twist of happiness. Human kind cannot bear too much happiness. *I* can't, that is to say, or so I have discovered. But I was going to tell you of my splendid idea.'

She had thought that when she met her father she would see why Meg had left him. The clash of personalities would have been obvious. But Charlotte could see no reason why the chemistry had not worked. She would have been the dominant partner, just as Daniel was the dominant partner in her own marriage, and Owen's life might have been different. There was nothing in their personalities, though, that necessitated a split. Time and chance had brought that about.

'You needn't say anything if you don't want to. I'm quite happy to sit here in silence,' she said. 'And then I must go.'

'You don't seem to wish to know what my idea is.'

'Yes, I do but I don't want you to tire yourself.'

He said there was no fear of that though he would be glad if she would fetch him a glass of water. 'My splendid idea is that your marriage should be blessed. I mean formally blessed by the church. We could have the ceremony in the college chapel. I have been thinking about it and can see no obstacle.'

'But we are properly married.'

'Speak to your husband about it. For me it would be a great pleasure to see your marriage blessed in the chapel where your mother and I were married.'

The meeting with her father slightly affected Charlotte's sense of balance. She was still the young professional woman with a thrusting husband but the ground under her had, just the tiniest bit, settled and become safer. She never had any secrets from Meg and would have told her about the trip to Oxford anyway but she told her, the next time they spoke on the telephone, with a bit more candour about the pleasure it had brought her.

'He's real handsome,' she said. 'And such fun.'

Meg was silent for so long that Charlotte thought they might have been cut off. 'Are you there, Meg? Can you hear me.'

'Yes, I'm here. This line is via satellite so there's the usual delay. What was that you were saying?'

'I saw my father.'

'I thought he was dead long ago. Did you ask about me? I hope you told him I was very happy.'

'He's so witty. He really made me laugh. His health is not good.'

'Don't tell me. He always fussed about his health. I

71

expect he's as stubborn as ever. He really was the most pig-headed man I have ever known and you can say that again. Made you laugh? You really are giving me news. Are you sure you saw the right man?'

'Sure. He told me about your wedding in the college chapel and about my christening.'

'I don't really want to talk about him, Charlotte. I suppose it was inevitable you would come together. So let's take your account of what happened as read.'

'He said I was christened in the family shawl and you probably have it. Is that so, Meg?' Satellite silence 'You don't know! But you must know. You can't let a christening shawl disappear like that.' Satellite silence. 'No, I'm not being silly. And Meg, he has this marvellous idea about Daniel and me. He thinks he can arrange for us to have our wedding blessed in a proper church ceremony and in the college chapel too, where you and he were married. Isn't that exciting? I haven't spoken to Daniel about it yet, he's in New York, but I'm sure he'll be as excited as I am. We spent some time in the chapel. There's no need for me to describe it because you will remember it only too well.'

Another pause, much longer than the usual satellite delay. 'He's a very determined man, Charlotte, not to say unscrupulous. Don't you see it's a way of getting his talons into your flesh? Oh, the things I could tell you about him. But carry on. Don't listen to me. Only don't ever say I didn't warn you. My love to Daniel. Goodbye for now.'

Daniel was away in New York longer than expected and Charlotte was still alone when her mother's letter arrived some days later.

Dear Charlotte,
    You took me by surprise when you called so I am

72

sure you will make allowance for my reaction and some of the things I said. I understand perfectly that you should wish to see your father and am sorry that he is in poor health but it is only to be expected at his age. He is much older than me. That was one consideration, but only one, that worked against our marriage. He always exaggerated his ailments and took to his bed on the slightest pretext. A little stomach ache would put him to bed for a week. He would think it was cancer and yet wouldn't send for the doctor for fear of being diagnosed. But as your grandmother used to say, he is like so many weak people, stubborn and tenacious.

It does not surprise me that he has this absurd idea of your going through a charade in the college chapel and I hope that Daniel will put his foot down. For your father it would not only be another church service – he is enthralled with ritual and I'm surprised he hasn't gone over to the Roman Catholic church, perhaps he has, you should find out – it would not only be the churchiness of the proceedings, it would be a way of revenging himself on me that would be the attraction. In the same chapel where we were married indeed! Didn't he blush when he made the proposal? But I do not wish to bore you with my caterwauling.

If you should see the man again do make it quite clear that my life with Simon has been blissfully happy and that if he has a bad conscience about the breakdown of our marriage he can set his mind at rest. I would not wish him to suffer unnecessarily.

All my love
Meg

P.S. It was not a shawl. It was a proper christening garment and I remember now that I gave it away some years ago to a charity that was collecting old clothes. With a little work it could be made into a dress for a toddler.

P.P.S. Why didn't you go to New York with Daniel? Then you could have come on here for a break which you well deserve. I do so wish we could be together for a while because I know how much that would boost your morale.

Daniel came back from New York in high spirits because what he had worked for seemed on the point of realisation: that Wheatley's in future would be known as Minotaur-Wheatley, that the chairman of Wheatley, Angus McIvor, would stand down to be replaced by another director, Percy Fitzroy, who was much favoured by Daniel, and that Daniel himself would be responsible for Forward Planning. It had been on the cards for Daniel to be chairman himself but the main Minotaur board thought it would be politic to respect Wheatley sensibilities by elevating a Wheatley man into the top job at the London end. The arrangement was interim but no advantage was seen in making this fact known to Fitzroy himself. The reality was that power lay with Forward Planning and Daniel was expected to make this clear in the document he was invited to prepare called 'Money Management for the Nineties: A Global Strategy.'

He was so euphoric about all this that when Charlotte told him of her visit to her father and what Meg thought of it he treated the news exuberantly. Owen sounded a real old gentleman and this idea he had for a service of blessing was grand. What an excuse for a party! He knew enough about Oxford to know the college could be paid to lay on the most splendid party in hall if it was out of term time and just think of the people they could invite! Percy Fitzroy and wife for two, that would be a gesture, then the Flooks to liven things up, the Clarke-Moodies – perhaps Cyril would sing, she was still in good voice – a few carefully chosen financial journalists and their spouses, they really would have a rave. Daniel saw no reason why Tomas shouldn't be there.

'Tomas?'

'Sure. The kid is just confused and an invitation like this is just what he needs to bring him out of his shell.'

'No way would that kid come. You underestimate him.'

'As for Meg, well I flatter myself I have a way with the old girl. I'll convince her. Not only that, she and Simon must come over for the ceremony. Why not? We're all grown up, aren't we?'

'You haven't seen Meg's letter yet.'

'Aw! She's O.K. really. Don't take what she says at face value.'

'Look, Daniel. Calm down. I don't know whether this service of blessing will actually take place yet. There may be technical reasons against it, either to do with the church or the college, and all Owen's doing for the time being is just finding out. But in any case we're having no big party. No rave. No big splash. All that is out!'

'No party?'

'A celebration drink, that's O.K. But nothing extravagant.'

'I don't know why not, honey. It's an occasion for rejoicing, isn't it? It wouldn't be a funeral.'

'Let's not talk about it until Owen lets us know whether the blessing is on. Even then I don't know that I would want to go through with it. Meg says it would be a charade and there's something in that. After all, we don't need a blessing. We're O.K. We're blessed already in my book. Our baby is the greatest blessing of all.'

After Daniel had read Meg's letter he laughed and said, 'I bet she's still in love with your father, even after all these years. There's real feeling in what she writes. Yeah, I know it reads a bit sharp but that's because she's stirred up. And why is she stirred up? She just feels the old romantic feeling. When I can get around to it I'll call her and tell her how much we love her. That's what she really wants to be told and if you can get some conciliatory remarks from Owen I guess I'd be happy to relay them. Shouldn't be too difficult if you tell him she's got kind, warm thoughts. Letters like Meg's get written but they have to be read between the lines. She's still hooked, if you ask me.'

Charlotte was able to take a firm line about the party because Owen had made her feel more at home with herself. More sure of herself. She got on well with Simon but there was always the knowledge he was not her real father and that made a difference between her and other kids who did have real fathers. Nothing to get worked up about, no more than sprang from the knowledge she did not look at all like Simon. About her background there was now no longer anything to be discovered. Whatever surprises Daniel might have thrown up at him she foresaw no surprises of her own. She could face the world with confidence, and that included Daniel.

Perhaps it was silly to get such a kick out of meeting Owen but she did not think so. Just to look at him had made her feel slightly different. *Her real father.* She owed life to this man; that meant, at the least, an inheritance of physical characteristics and, since it was hard to draw a line between them and personality, a certain style. She was shifted, just the tiniest bit, out of her mother Meg's aura and into an awareness of Owenish strands in her own make-up. She had just loved being shown Oxford by him and could not think that Meg, in her position, would have responded at all.

In the same way Tomas must have been changed by the meeting with his own father, though Charlotte could not have said how. Paternity counted. Tomas's cussedness may have owed something to Daniel. She could imagine Daniel's bounce turning into that sort of defiance if he found himself hedged in; and that is how Tomas saw himself, hedged in by a relationship he had been dropped into just at the moment he was stretching his wings in new freedom.

And what of Meg? What did she owe to her own father? She had once told Charlotte that before he died he let it be known that she would not be welcome at his funeral, he was so angry with her for running off with 'that American.' This was comical because Grandpa seemed to think that even when dead he would be sufficiently in evidence to welcome or rebuff his mourners. Like father like daughter. This was a grand illusion that Meg too could well have entertained about herself.

'One thing Meg's right about,' said Daniel. 'You could do with a break. Let's pack a bag and go off to Paris for a few days.'

So to Paris they went where Charlotte discovered Daniel had business appointments to keep and she did sight-seeing alone. They had a splendid dinner at the Tour d'Argent, though, and Daniel hired a car and drove to Chartres where she took a lot of photographs. Much to Daniel's disappointment there was no production at the Paris Opera House. Paris was just shut down for the vacation, he said, and Charlotte was reminded of the way Owen had said Oxford was deserted. Both places were full of tourists.

One of the consequences of Daniel landing the Forward Planning assignment was their stay in London would be much longer than expected. At the clinic Charlotte had been told there was every chance her baby would be a boy and no sooner did Daniel know this than he said they would have to make a decision about where the boy would be born. They talked about this on and off for days and they were still talking about it in Paris. They were sitting at a table out on the pavement, the canopied territory of a cafe near the Opera, when the talk came near to being a quarrel.

No matter where Alexander James Blair was born – they had already decided his name – he would be an American citizen but if he was born in London he could be British as well. Double nationality might be a bonus. He might decide to live in the UK, particularly if Washington had another call-up. Charlotte said that if there was a national emergency she would not want the boy dodging the draft and the argument about what Alexander James might do in the 21st century became sharp. Daniel said he'd have to check but he had an idea that if the kid had double nationality he'd have to opt for one or the other when he was eighteen and naturally he would choose to go along with his parents. In any case he would make his own decision. So it was all an argument about nothing. Charlotte wanted to put temptation out of Alexander James's way by going to the States for her confinement.

'Honey, whatever you say. This is a matter in which you're the boss. Let's not get worked up.' Daniel waved an arm to attract the waiter's attention. 'That's as near as we've got to disagreement on something important. Now

78

that it is happily resolved I guess we go and buy something.'

The something turned out to be earrings with a corona of small diamonds round a ruby the size of a hazel nut which they found in a Rue de la Paix jeweller's. Charlotte wanted to wear them immediately but the jeweller would not accept a cheque, he wanted a banker's draft in francs. This involved a trip to the American Express office and a delay of a couple of days before Charlotte could look at herself in the mirror with these glorious earrings in place.

'Daniel, they're really wonderful. The diamonds just crackle with light. I didn't know there was such a glow as you have from these rubies. I look at them and I feel myself sinking in, like into fire. See? When I move the head the earrings are living things. Oh, you are a darling.' And she pulled him down for a kiss.

'One day we'll tell Alexander James how you had them.'

Surprisingly, Charlotte did not find in Paris lipstick the exact match to her rubies and had to wait until they returned to London. She could not wear the earrings in public without this special lipstick. When she did Daniel thought the effect was quite stunning; the rubies did something to her eyes, made them a warmer brown, and this is how he wanted her to look when she next saw her father. Charlotte was against this. She sensed that Owen would not like such flamboyance and in any case the earrings were for evening wear and certainly not right for the first meeting of Owen with his son-in-law in that plain and sober Oxford flat.

Owen had established there was no obstacle to a ceremony of blessing in the college chapel provided it was performed before term started. He would have liked to conduct the service himself but on reflection had come to the conclusion he was not up to it; the older he became the more emotional he was. This was a circumstance, he said on the telephone to Charlotte, that he found as interesting as it was surprising. Not that he was really old, only just turned seventy, but he was old enough to know something of the passions of age, as he described them, when the memories of what might have been come to the surface. The college chaplain, Tim Westbrook, was back from Greece and would be glad to take the service.

Daniel was listening on the spare phone. 'Tell him,' he hissed to Charlotte with his hand over the phone, 'we'd really like him to conduct the service. It would be much more fun.'

'We'll talk more about it when we meet on Thursday, Owen,' she said. 'Goodbye for now. Take care.'

Len drove them down. Daniel had wanted to take Owen out to lunch but Owen insisted on playing host. Mrs Springer was perfectly capable of providing what was necessary and he would be all the more effective as a host because – and he did not know how much of a surprise this would be – his sister Eleanor, Charlotte's aunt, would be present too. Yes, this was a surprise because Charlotte did not even know of Aunt Eleanor's existence.

Owen shouted from a window when they arrived, saying, 'Come on up. You know the way,' and there she was, obviously Aunt Eleanor, to hold open the door of the flat for them and say, 'You must be Shar and you must be Daniel. Call me, quite simply, aunt. It will be the first time in my life I have been so addressed because you were too young for it before you went away, Shar. Your father and I have no other siblings so you have no cousins. You are, as my niece, unique.'

Dressed in a white blouse with a loosely tied and huge silk cravat patterned with poppies and cornflowers, she

80

held them at the door until she had finished what she had to say. Her greyish-yellow hair was silky too and caught up in a severe knot at the back of her head.

'Come in! Come in!' Owen shouted gaily and pranced forward, still in his blue blazer. 'Shar, my dear, may I kiss you on the cheek? And you, Mr Blair, I shake by the hand.'

'Daniel is the name, sir, and I have to say it is a privilege to meet you.'

'Sherry now. Dry or medium? I commend this Tio Pepe.'

The serving was done by Eleanor who brought in the iced vichyssoise. While Owen and Daniel chatted Charlotte helped with the salmon mayonnaise and new potatoes. Later there were strawberries and cream, though Owen took yoghourt instead of the cream because of his diet. Then stilton and biscuits. Owen invited Daniel to open and serve the Sancerre. It was a splendid summer lunch and Charlotte could only guess at the trouble it had given.

Owen had not realised Daniel had been a Rhodes scholar and so no stranger to Oxford. But Daniel had stuck it for only a year, he said. He had to get home and earn some money. He guessed he'd been a disappointment to his college.

They drank toasts to mark the reunion. Daniel proposed a toast to the unborn Alexander and, as she drank, Charlotte wondered what Meg would make of it all. What did it matter? This was the world Meg had broken away from and there was no more to be said. Life had its fractures and its patchings up and she hoped to God nothing would ever come between her and Daniel. From the beginning she had known that he liked women and the existence of Tomas had come as no shock. She did wish, though, he wasn't so cocky about Tomas. She would kick his ankle if he so much as mentioned him at this get-together. Nobody brought up Meg's name until Eleanor did and Charlotte saw by the way she called her Margaret and not Meg she was capable of making trouble. It was the disapproving way she said Margaret.

Apropos nothing at all, as though the matter really weighed on her mind she said, 'You know without doubt, Shar, that your mother Margaret – I gather she is still alive – and your father were never divorced. He does not accept divorce and neither do I.'

Charlotte said there must be some mistake but she was sure there had been a divorce. Otherwise Meg and Simon could not have married, could they?

'That must have been just an American divorce of some sort, if it took place, but it would not have been a divorce under English law.'

'Since my mother is an American citizen and lives in the States I guess that won't concern her.' Charlotte decided she did not like Aunt Eleanor.

'But it concerns your father,' said Eleanor. 'Doesn't it, Owen?'

Talking about it afterwards Daniel said this was the moment when he decided to turn on the charm. Eleanor was a dragon, perhaps, but he was going to tame her. She would be eating out of his hand. To that end he had dropped the Aunt and addressed her simply as Eleanor which he said was a lovely name and if ever Charlotte and he had a daughter, which they very much hoped for, Eleanor was a name that would certainly figure on their list of possibles. He was of British stock, Scottish in particular, and Eleanor was a name big in British history. Wasn't it interesting how you either liked or disliked a name because of the people you knew who were called by it? Yes, for sure, Eleanor was a name that went down on their list.

'I've never reconciled myself,' said Eleanor, 'to this new practice of calling everyone by their first names on first acquaintance. In hospital my brother was called Owen even by the ordinary nurses.'

Owen said he did not like it either but he had put up with being called by his first name because he knew it was well meant; and after all one's Christian name was one's real name, the one given in baptism. He found it more difficult to call the nurses by their first names. It made them, without their surnames, curiously unidentifiable. But what he really wanted to talk about was the service of blessing. Did Shar and Daniel mean to go ahead with it? He had a feeling he might have bullied them into the idea.

'Not at all,' said Daniel. 'It really made my day and Charlotte's day when I heard of it. We'd love to. But we'd like it to be a quiet occasion.'

Owen nodded happily. 'That makes the point that I had in mind. You do appreciate that although it is not a marriage service it is nevertheless a service in which the celebrants make the usual solemn vows?'

'No, I hadn't thought about it.' Charlotte would have hated to confess it but at important moments she had a habit of silently consulting Meg. Even Meg did not know this. Charlotte attached a lot of importance to Meg's approval or disapproval and she now remembered her warning about the blessing. 'I mean what vows are we talking about?'

'The usual ones about loving and honouring until death do you part. They are very solemn. They are made in the sight of God himself.'

So they were the same vows her father and mother had made and now there was the prospect of making them with Daniel at the very spot, in the same chapel. Everyone waited, particularly Aunt Eleanor it seemed, for Charlotte's comment and when it came Daniel gasped and put down his glass. Owen and Eleanor said nothing. It was more than that, it was a special silence they created that went on and on and in which Charlotte listened to the big clock with a front like a Greek temple that ticked away in a corner.

'We shall have to think about it. I hadn't realised there were vows. It seems to me that not many people can be so certain about themselves or what's going to happen.' It might even have been Meg talking.

'Without the vows,' said Eleanor, first to break the long silence, 'the ceremony would be a charade.' Which with a start, Charlotte realised, was the word that Meg had used herself.

'They are holy vows,' said Owen. 'I'm glad you realise the solemnity of them. To break them is a grave offence.'

Before they left he said, 'Write to me. Telephone if you must but the telephone makes me nervous.'

In the car, on the way back to London, Charlotte said they could not possibly go on with the ceremony of blessing after what was said. It would be too much in the shadow of her parents' marriage service. She could imagine Aunt Eleanor's sceptical bearing and her father's mixture of rejoicing and sadness over what he had called memories of what might have been. Her decision – and that is what it amounted to – had nothing to do with Daniel. They were already united in the vows made in the mayor's office, they would honour them so far as was humanly possible, but they could not do more.

'I didn't know you were all that religious, Charlotte. You don't go to church.'

'Perhaps I'd better start.'

84

Daniel was too much caught up with Minotaur-Wheatley affairs to dwell on his disappointment but he referred to it from time to time, oddly enough in connection with Tomas. The kid would have been interested to see Oxford. Meeting the rest of the family would thaw him out. Perhaps they could think up some other occasion. How about Wagner? Wouldn't it be great if he turned out to be a fan and they could take him to the autumn Ring cycle at Covent Garden?

3
Tomas

Once a year, usually in the spring, when the horse chestnut trees were in blossom, classes would have an outing, often into the country but sometimes to go sightseeing in the city of Prague itself. On one of these outings Tomas saw the Josefov district for the first time. It was the old Jewish quarter and it caught his imagination. He took trips to the Josefov district by himself, particularly when he was at the Gymnasium, and inspected the synagogues that had been turned into museums. Here were temple curtains, candelabra, old books, shawls, horn trumpets and wooden tablets inscribed with the strange Hebrew lettering – the same lettering he saw on the clock of the Jewish Town Hall. He often went to the Old Jewish cemetery and clambered over the uneven ground to look at the gravestones. The place was at its best in winter when the stones were capped with snow and caked on one side where the wind had driven it.

All his mother Vera would tell him about his father was

that he was dead. His step-father Karel and his two young step-brothers, Stepan and Vilem, loved him as a proper father and brothers should and he was not to bother his head about someone who was no longer with them. Tomas did, though, and the idea that his dead father was a Jew took hold. What other explanation could there be for Vera making such a mystery out of what would otherwise be perfectly straightforward? She would not even tell him what his real name was. His father had been killed in some trouble after the Russians came back and that was the end of the matter. This did not rule out the possibility he was a Jew because not all Jews had been taken away and murdered by the Nazis. Tomas got it into his head that his father had died in Prague and was buried in that old graveyard. Even when he was told no one had been buried there for nearly two hundred years Tomas still believed this.

He took time off from the Gymnasium to take part in the Youth Theatre productions because there was nothing he loved more than acting. Pretending to be somebody else was a wonderful escape. He ceased being Tomas Rais and became successively a soldier, a deceitful priest, a drunken aristocrat and, in the Youth Theatre's greatest production, the lean and hungry looking Cassius in *Julius Caesar*. He caught the eye of Karl Jacubek and was invited to take the part of the Fool in the Obelisk Theatre production of *King Lear*. This turned out to be the great emotional experience of his life so far and when, because of this production, The Obelisk was shut down and Jacubek found himself behind bars, Tomas felt life drain out of him. It was no consolation to be chosen for a Youth Theatre visit, with a production of a modern and politically correct play, to London. He did not like the play or enjoy acting in it. He was still rocked by the storms of

Lear and anything less stirring was trivial indeed. Its banning in Prague was one of the reasons why on impulse he walked into the police station opposite the Old Yard Theatre and asked for political asylum.

The Karl Jacubek *Lear* had been in modern dress. Everyone was in military uniform and Lear himself had a moustache very like Stalin's. He also smoked a pipe. Jo Susta played him for all he was worth as the mad old tyrant; Regan, Goneril and their husbands were the ruthless dissidents that a rule of terror can breed, Cordelia seemed to stand for Dubcek's kind of liberalism and, like Dubcek, suffered the consequences. The Fool? Without telling Jacubek Tomas played him as a Jew. Only by thinking of the Fool as a Jew could he strike the right note of desperate alienation from the rest of that mad world. *Lear* did not lend itself to the kind of political interpretation Jacubek intended and he well knew it. The uniforms, the moustache and the pipe smoking were superficial touches but they were enough to bring in the police.

When Tomas learned that the Old Yard Theatre was to stage its own production of *King Lear* he was much struck by the coincidence and excited at the thought of having a hand in it. Everyone in the company, even a trainee stage-manager, could attend script meetings where policy was decided on. Those who came listened with interest to Tomas's account of the Prague production. Fred Bean, the artistic director, said modern dress was out, it would only trivialise the myth. What he had in mind was a *Lear* contemporary with Shakespeare but set in the Scottish Highlands where a feudal society still existed, and clan chiefs had their own armies, with plaids, trews, broadswords and bagpipes.

Fred named a well-known actor currently featuring in a TV soap who would be glad to take on *Lear* just for the kudos. He'd do it for peanuts in a limited run which was all Fred intended anyway. And don't let this TV performance make you think he wasn't a fine classical actor too! He did TV for the money but *Lear* would massage his reputation. And just his name would sell tickets.

Tomas approached him after the meeting and asked whether he could be auditioned for the Fool. 'No way,' said Fred. 'You've not got an Equity card and without that nobody sets foot on a British stage in either joy or anger. What's more you're not a British subject and that rules the card out for you anyway. How do you get a card? Don't think I'm being funny but it's only after you've done some performances. And how do you get the performances, you ask. The profession's overcrowded, mate.'

'What is Equity?'

But Fred was answering the phone and dismissing Tomas with a wave of the hand.

When asking for a rise Tomas discovered that his pay as trainee stage-manager came not from the theatre but from the Arts Council and was not only fixed with no possibility of any increase but was temporary, for another six months and no more. After that he'd have to find a proper job. On his money he could not exist and moonlighted as a waiter in a Notting Hill restaurant until he was given a part time contract with the Czech radio service at Bush House, the External Services of the BBC, reading translated extracts in 'What the Papers say', mainly because he had a good voice and accent. He made an impression with his knowledge of Dickens and Conrad on a man in the Hebrew service called Josh Smilan, who was Israel-born, a sabra, and whose grandparents on both sides had come from Russia. He and Tomas sat in the Bush House canteen for hours, talking about theatre in Israel, Middle East politics, Central European politics, religion, English literature – Josh could quote poetry at length – about Shakespeare, *King Lear* in particular, and about Tomas's belief that his father had been a Jew.

Josh laughed. 'It's a common fantasy. People are always turning up at Tel-Aviv airport claiming that they are Jewish when in fact they are not. They'd have a right to domicile in Israel if they were but that has nothing to do with the claim they make. They've a perfectly good domicile already in the UK or the States or France or wherever. No, they are living out a fantasy. They see themselves as Jewish. It seems – well, not exactly romantic, it would be silly to say that, but for some obscure reason they want to identify with a people who've had such a hell of a time. Maybe a yearning for kinship. Have you been circumcised? No. You probably didn't have a Jewish dad but you want to belong.'

'That is the exact opposite of what I feel. I've no feeling for the tribe. I walk by myself, no father, no mother, no brothers. I've no loyalties to anything but my own self-interest. I reject political parties and statism. The only thing I really want to do is act and pretend I'm somebody else.'

'You're a nihilist.'

'Is that what it's called?'

'You deceive yourself, Tomas. If you're a nihilist I'd have thought this fantasy of a Jewish father was something you could do without.'

'Who is the real me? I don't know. Perhaps this fantasy as you call it is another way of saying no to the real me and becoming somebody else. The only way to make life tolerable is pretending and acting. But deep down, the real me is somebody who just rejects.'

'Why?'

Tomas shrugged. 'I don't feel I'm a bastard. Nobody can call me that.'

'And your father was a Jew?'

'Yes.'

'Perhaps the real you rejects the idea of being a Jew.'

Not for a long time, after many meetings and much talk, did Tomas tell Josh about the American, Mr Blair, who has unexpectedly appeared and claimed to be his father and that he was a bastard. Josh was amazed.

'I don't believe him. I'm not a bastard. It is a trick of my mother's to get money out of him.'

'Here, wait a minute son. Let's go into this a little more carefully.'

The resulting conversation in the canteen clatter, while other eaters pushed past, and after Josh had returned from the queue with more coffee, caused Tomas to write to his mother. He had previously written only briefly and she, apart from a long letter at the beginning of his stay urging him to return home, had been brief too. For all his fluency in English, writing Czech came much more easily and he wrote more fully and perhaps more candidly than he had intended.

After a conventional opening he went on to mention the American, Mr Daniel Blair, for the first time and to say he had been much distressed by what he had said. His wife, though, was charming. Had things been different she might have become a real friend.

'When you originally wrote and said Mr Blair was my father I could only wonder why, if this was true, you had not told me before. It was not for want of asking you. Without real knowledge the imagination takes over and I will not disguise from you ideas came to me. I believed you when you said my father was dead but who he had been was what my imagination played upon. Perhaps it is foolish to wonder about one's parentage. We are just creatures crawling between earth and sky. To ask whence we came or why is vanity. Having been led so far I am in need of more information to feed this vanity. Or my anxieties. Even neurosis. To be blunt, you must write in such a way that you lay to rest my suspicions that what you have told me is only to conceal some more disagreeable truth. How and where could you have met this American? I know you were in London on a diplomatic posting but you are not a person for casual adventures. I have to tell you frankly I do not like this man and do not wish to see him again. But you must be more specific about the background to the story you told.'

In due course a letter came back in her familiar green ink with the little drawings of comic faces in the margin: a circle with two dots for eyes, a little circle for the nose and a semi-circle for the mouth to show gloom, turned the other way up for merriment. A pin woman walked to show how she went shopping and how difficult it was to find what she wanted. Another pin woman lifted her arms high to show joy at hearing from her dear Tomas. And so on.

'But to be equally direct with you, my son, you seem in your letter to be unaware of your implication that I had invented Daniel Blair. Why? How do you think I ever knew of his existence? It is wicked to imply that your real father is someone else and that I had named Daniel almost at hazard, being just a man I had met and there was no more to the story than that. Reflect on this absurdity. The truth is that I loved him and he is indeed your father though it is a miracle that you have met each other for I thought he must be in America. His gain is my loss. I wrote to him on impulse fearing you might be friendless and destitute and that he would make contact with you across the Atlantic. The news that I gave him must have come as a shock because he would not have known of your existence. It was likely that he would reject you. I had to face that possibility but the harshness of circumstances dictated that the risk had to be taken.'

And so on. It showed more affection than he had expected. She had never demonstrated any love for him or even a liking, compared that is to say with the hugs and kisses she gave to his half-brothers. He had once heard her say to a neighbour, 'Tomas I do not really understand. He keeps his thoughts to himself.' It was true that on the rare occasions she kissed him he found it impossible not to stiffen and lean away. In the family it seemed to be accepted that he was not to be made a fuss of; he was too independent and bookish to need any great show of love but the fact was he needed it desperately and was jealous of Stephan and Vilem. He received more good-humoured tenderness from his step-father Karel than he did from his mother and the boys always rushed out joyfully to meet him when he came home from High School or the theatre. But it was not the same. He wanted his mother's face to light up at the sight of him and it never did.

Alone one day in Fred Bean's office Tomas was tempted to pick up the phone and ring her in Prague. Fred's was the only phone in the building that did not go through the theatre switchboard. By direct dialling he could be through to her number in seconds and talking to her. But what would he say? That her letter had touched him? That if she had shown to him in person the concern of her letter he might not be where he was now, among strangers in a foreign land? He put his hand on the receiver. The line would undoubtedly be tapped in Prague and a call from London might compromise her, no matter how personal and innocuous. So he let the temptation pass, withdrew his hand and went out of the building, as far as King's Cross station where he stood on the concourse watching the train indicators. Watford, Leeds, York, Newcastle-upon-Tyne, Edinburgh, the names were thrown up by the chattering indicators. He would like to go to these places. Just to pronounce their names, as he did to himself, calmed him down. Funny sort of comfort, he thought, for not calling his mother, but that is what the station and its noises provided.

'Where the hell have you been?' Back at the theatre Fred met him on the stairs, having sent out his secretary to look in vain for Tomas. 'You're supposed to be up at the warehouse. Get cracking boy.'

The old warehouse was a mile away and the place where scenery, costumes and other props were stored. It was where Tomas spent most of his time and Fred was quite right, he should be over there checking stuff that had come in from the costumiers. Jock the carpenter and Ian the electrician gave him a round of applause when he climbed into the back of their truck.

During rehearsals for *Lear* Tomas struck up a friendship with Justin Wragg, an actor who claimed to have done everything – straight, the northern club scene, bit parts in TV, provincial rep, a spell with the Royal Shakespeare Company, and now never went anywhere without his silver flask of Scotch malt whisky. He seemed relaxed and sleepy eyed most of the time. He had enemies, among them Mike, the General Manager, who said he'd had unfortunate experiences with Wragg before and warned Fred against using him. Fred, though, had a soft spot for Wragg and said O.K. he was an alcoholic but he'd known worse and old Justin had style. Justin Wragg was to be Lear's Fool.

'You've got to be a bit of an acrobat to play the Fool. I

95

could do it one time because that's how I was trained. Michel St Denis. You heard of him? Great man of the theatre. When he gave me an audition he made me stand on my head. For him actors had to be all rounders. Sing, dance, the lot. He said that's how Shakespeare's own company were. Every tragedy ended up with a jig. I'm past it now, to be honest. But I can still show a good leg and hop about, especially if I keep off the hard stuff.'

Tomas observed closely the way he moved and spoke in rehearsals. From the Czech text for the Fool he moved easily to the English and while Wragg was busy on the stage Tomas stood in the wings mouthing and gesticulating in the part.

Fred caught him one day and said, 'What are you playing at? Your job is giving Jock a hand. Get moving! No, wait a minute.'

He appeared to have second thoughts and went on stage for a word with Julian Spiers, who was playing Lear in singlet and shorts. He beckoned Wragg over. After some minutes of talk, during which Lear and the Fool looked in Tomas's direction, Fred came back and said, 'You think you're so clever. Get out there and do that coxcomb bit.'

Old Yard productions were mounted as cheaply as possible, with a lot of doubling and as few understudies as Fred thought he could get away with. If Lear went sick the show would close. For some of the other characters actors in the company would be expected to step in and Fred was even prepared to go on stage and read from a script himself if all else failed. The Fool was special, though. Not everyone could manage that coarse mixture of cheek and servility, particularly when it involved scampering about and singing. Tomas immediately realised he was being tried out as an understudy and that Wragg did not like the idea at all.

'What about Equity?' asked Tomas.

'Just get on with it, son.'

Wragg walked off the stage but Lear entered into the fun of the experiment and roared, 'How now, my pretty knave! How dost though?'

'Sirrah, you were best take my coxcomb.' Tomas plunged in with spirit but he was less word perfect than he thought and Lear took to prompting him and making encouraging noises.

'Take a deep breath, boy. Don't rush it. You're doing fine.' He had a whip which he cracked noisily. 'Dost call me fool, boy?'

Lear switched easily from being prompter and encourager to being Lear himself and somehow they struggled through the scene as far as the entry of Goneril when Fred came back on stage and said that would be enough for the time being.

Tomas was impressed with the seriousness the actors went to work, even in rehearsal. Compared to what they were doing the Obelisk players had been playacting. Lear, though, his daughters, even Justin Wragg, threw themselves into their parts with such vehemence and conviction the bare rehearsal stage took on some of the qualities of Lear's palace. They seemed to believe they were the characters they played. And yet in a matter of minutes they could drop the grand manner and, when Fred called a break, behave like ordinary human beings.

In one of these breaks Tomas spoke to Julian about the switching, who seemed not to understand what he was saying. 'Lear's an impossible old trout, sure.'

Extraordinary that a man who played Lear should call him a trout. If you did not take him seriously how could you play the part with such conviction? Tomas found it

97

difficult to put his question into words and ended up by asking Julian if he had a favourite role.

Julian did not take the question seriously and after some moments of pretended thought said, 'You talking about Shakespeare? We-e-e-l, Julius Caesar's a good part. He disappears half way through and you go home. Or you could if it weren't for the curtain calls.'

'But don't you just sink yourself into a part? And some parts are easier for you than others?'

'I see what you're getting at.'

'I mean you want to become the character you play?'

'To become Lear? I'd be leary of that, mate. I'd be leary of any actor who confused himself with the part he was playing.'

Six weeks of rehearsals and Tomas spent a lot of that time in the warehouse, some of it helping the sound engineers make a tape for the storm scene. At signals he had to shake metal sheeting to simulate thunder and work a wind machine. Fred was there with a stop watch relating the effects to text. Lightning flashes were the electrician's job and came later, when they moved into the theatre. For rain Fred wanted real water, jetted from high up under pressure and it was Tomas's job to climb into the flies and fix the sprays. No scenery to speak of, just massive chairs and a cyclorama screen where clouds appeared to race but sometimes stopped when the mechanism stuck. Early in rehearsals Wragg handed his silver flask over to Mike, the General Manager, saying he wouldn't touch a drop from that moment on. Mike put it in his office from where it disappeared and Wragg, by delivering his lines with portentous gestures and an exaggerated drawl, was accused by Fred of being drunk. He was wearing a huge bonnet and a kilt that came down to his ankles. This did not stop him from standing on his head, as Michel St Denis had requested, and showing the blue football shorts he wore underneath. Fred pulled Wragg off and sent Tomas on to see if there was any hope of using him for the Fool.

'You scratch about like an old hen,' he said. 'Use your legs. When you turn don't just stagger round in the way you were doing. Point your right toe forward first. That's right. Now, show you're really frightened of that whip. Lear isn't making an empty threat. Remember, he's a killer.'

At the dress rehearsal Wragg was drunk again though not so drunk he was unable to cope. There were two previews when the public came in with cheap tickets and no press were allowed. Wragg managed those all right but on the real first night he attacked Lear with his broadsword and Fred told Tomas to take over, dressed just as he was in jeans and trainers but wearing the bonnet snatched from Wragg's head. They were out on the heath with the storm raging, thunder rolling, lightning flashing and the water slashing down from Tomas's sprays in a general confusion that Fred must have been counting on to obscure the oddity of Tomas's appearance and his other shortcomings. Lear bellowed, Tomas squeaked and as Fred had cut the main piece still left to him, the Merlin prophecy, Tomas was left little to say in that particular scene but the one line, 'This is a brave night to cool a courtesan,' which he delivered centre stage and alone.

He was within feet of the first row of the stalls where he suddenly spied a man with an expanse of white shirting and a bow tie looking at him with a grin. He had already sung the little song about the rain it raineth every day but the sight of this man so startled him he remained where he was and, having to do something, sang the song again. The man laughed and clapped, the woman at his side started to clap too, others in the audience joined in so

Tomas bowed out to the first applause he had received in an English theatre. The man was Mr Blair and the woman was Charlotte.

Tomas did not doubt they had come along not just for the first night but to see him. But how could they have known he would appear when he did not even know himself? Only Fred knew. But did even he know before Wragg started laying about with that broadsword? Old mental habits stirred. He was not going to be paranoiac about the appearance of the Blairs; this was London and not Prague, where unexpected coincidences of this sort made one suspect that the police were at the bottom of the mystery, that behind one's back plots were being made. What plot could someone in the theatre – maybe Fred himself, or Mike the General Manager – be involved in with Daniel Blair? And was Daniel Blair himself just what he made himself out to be?

After the show Tomas slipped on a jacket and went round to meet the Blairs as they came out of the theatre. Daniel was overjoyed to see him and said, 'We were in on your triumph, Tomas. Charlotte will always remember your triumph. Champagne is called for. Look, we've got the car so why not come back and drink that champagne. We owe it to you.'

'Yes, do come, Tomas,' said Charlotte. 'It would make us so happy.'

'How did you know I was to be in the show?'

'Ah!' Daniel laughed and put a hand on his shoulder. 'News gets around.'

'I want to ask you something.'

'That's fine. Hop in or we'll be trampled under by this crowd. Good show. You were the star, Tomas. No doubt about it at all.'

What Tomas needed to ask was so compelling that in

100

spite of his doubts and even hostility towards Daniel he agreed to go back to the flat and drink champagne, his clothes still wet from the artificial rain. Once he had overcome his terror at being thrust on to the stage in front of an audience Tomas had been able to take a grip of himself only by remembering the Fool was a Jew. That was how Tomas had played him in Prague and now, in London, the Jew came to his rescue. He, the Jew, was threatened by the whip and joked about it, to be hanged at the last. That is to say, he Tomas, was threatened.

Daniel made the opening of the champagne bottle into a performance. He opened a window so that the cork could fly out into the street, cheering it on its way and prompting cheers from passers-by in the street below. Charlotte and Daniel drank to Tomas. Then he, too, took a glass. And another glass. Daniel opened another bottle and once more shot the cork into the street. It was a warm, humid evening. The street lights and the lights from the houses opposite were softened by the moist air. Somewhere a piano was being played clumsily and Tomas could make out what was being attempted, a Schubert impromptu which his step-father often played. The warmth and the music, not to speak of the champagne, lifted Tomas out of London into a stranger city where people laughed all the time, danced, acted, rejoiced and were kind to each other.

'Now what was it you wanted to ask me, Tomas?'

Daniel stood with his legs apart while Charlotte and Tomas sat on the grand well-padded blue and white settee. On the stage Tomas had thought the night was blossoming into a really great night that he would have liked to share with old friends back in Prague. Instead, after his triumph – he had come to believe what Daniel said – he

101

was here, drinking champagne where he did not really want to be and feeling as drunk as Wragg looked.

'Are you a Jew, Mr Biair?'

'No. What makes you think I might be?'

'It is important for me to know. I want the truth.'

Daniel squatted, as truth was on the carpet and needed closer examination. 'The truth is no. Why do you ask?'

'Because if you were a Jew then I would be a Jew and I've always suspected I might be.'

'Nothing like that.' Daniel was amused. 'Is that what you're afraid of, being a Jew?'

'Afraid? No. You are sure of what you are saying?'

'Absolutely. My father wasn't a churchgoer but he regarded himself as a member of the Presbyterian church in Albany. My mother was a Baptist and that is how I was brought up. They are your grandparents. Look, Tomas. I'd have been proud to be a Jew but I have to tell you that if you think you're one then it would be because your mother was.'

'Impossible.'

'Then forget it.'

Tomas persisted. 'One of your grandparents might have been Jewish and you knew nothing about it.'

'No, Tomas. Impossible. It would be great to have Jewish blood but I haven't. It looks as though you haven't either.'

Tomas slept in the spare bedroom and woke with a hangover to find that Daniel had already left for the office and Charlotte gave him coffee and fresh croissants which she had popped out to buy from a local baker. In the first moments of waking he thought the happenings of the night before might have been a dream. He had been whisked up into paradise and then dropped into an abyss of disappointment and disillusion. That could not have been what really happened. But it could. He looked at himself in the mirror wearing a pair of Daniel's scarlet and gold pyjamas. What Daniel said came back and hurt. He took a shower but decided not to shave with the electric razor Charlotte offered him. He had shaved for more than a year but now he would grow a beard as a protest against the truths Daniel had rubbed into him. He did not doubt they were truths.

Charlotte extracted something of his feelings and said, 'I can't understand why you're so upset at not being a Jew.'

'I shall go to Israel and work on a kibbutz. Then I shall marry an Israeli girl and our son will be a Jew.' The thought cheered him and he even laughed. 'It'll be hard to give up the idea I was really somebody else because that was a great comfort to me. I shall be happy with my Jewish son. Then I shall recover something of the old feeling. Not quite, perhaps. At least I shall think of myself as not one person but two.'

'That's how I feel now that I am pregnant.'

'You are pregnant? May God grant you a good delivery.'

Charlotte took the crockery into the kitchen and called back. 'I don't think it's just being pregnant. It's been coming on some time, this idea somebody else inside was talking to me.'

'It sounds as though we may have something in common.'

Tomas did not play Lear's Fool again because Wragg was sacked from the cast and a new man from the National Theatre brought in. The production had been well received and House Full notices went up. At the script meeting there was talk of extending the run and even transferring to a big West End Theatre. This would bring money to the Old Yard and Fred was grateful to Tomas because he had not made such a botch of his first night performance that the critics could seize on it as an excuse to pan the whole production. Tomas was given a bonus. It encouraged him to move out of his shabby room in Praed Street to a bed-sitter off Westbourne Grove where he had a view of trees that gave the illusion he was in touch with the country.

That first night, followed by the celebration with the Blairs, was Tomas's time of change. It was brought about not so much by what happened on stage or by the effect of champagne and Daniel's assurance he was not a Jew as by the dream that followed. He was back in the old house in Prague where the floorboards of his bedroom creaked and he was being led by Charlotte as through a minefield. Only at certain places did the floorboards creak. By remembering where they were and stepping carefully he could move all the way from his bed to the door without making a sound. In his dream he made mistakes in spite of Charlotte's attempts to guide him. This was all the more agonising because he knew that if he did tread on a squeaking board it would attract the attention of Fred who would want to know why he, as the Fool, was wearing the coxcomb cap and not the Scottish bonnet.

Going through a dream like that was like going through some initiation rite. He had learned something. Just what he would have been hard put to say. He hadn't warmed to Daniel and had been shocked by Daniel's assumption he'd be pleased to learn he had no Jewish blood but the original hostility had evaporated, thanks in the main to Charlotte who put it plainly when they next met that he ought to take a hold on himself and realise he was what he was and not a puppet.

'A puppet?'

'Yes. You're young. You don't have to be looking over

your shoulder all the time. The past is the past and maybe the future will be different. Maybe you can help to make it different. You've never said why you asked for political asylum. I'd have thought things were on the move in Eastern Europe the way you'd like them to move. Gorbachov seems almost too good to be true. If there's *glasnost* in Russia why shouldn't there be a loosening up in Prague too?'

'A puppet?'

'Sure. I can see you've some hang up about being Jewish.'

This was at the buffet lunch in the theatre where Charlotte, unabashed by her previous reception, had tracked Tomas down after he had failed to get in touch as promised. Nobody questioned her presence; even Mike the General Manager, who had made trouble, was relaxed about her being there. That was because Tomas was obviously glad to see her which could only mean that she was not some prying official. Other days they met in Kensington Gardens which seemed a favourite place with Charlotte. It was here, sitting on a bench, that Tomas started talking about Solzhenitsyn, whom he heard of in Prague but not read. Now he had read *The First Circle* and *The Gulag Archipelago*, books Charlotte had not read either, so he passed her the grubby English-translation paperbacks which he had borrowed from the Bush House library.

'You don't feel he's a strange sort of person?' she asked some time later when she returned the books.

'Strange? No, he seems a good man.'

'That's what I mean. He was born in 1918 so he's a complete product of the Soviet system yet he writes as though he had been brought up in, say, Paris.'

105

'You could say I'm a complete product of the system in Czechoslovakia. That doesn't mean I'm not human.'

Solzhenitzyn did not seem strange to Tomas because although he knew nothing at first hand about the camps he did know what it was like to live in a police state and thought he would have written as Solzhenitzyn did if only he'd had those experiences, his gifts as a writer, and his courage; which was asking a lot.

'There are lots of people who think like Solzhenitzyn. They don't feel part of the system. Slav peoples, like the Russians and the Czechs, are not like Germans. They always see distance between themselves and the state. The state and the police and the apparatchiks are different from us. You might get police states but you don't get policed people. Not all the time. At least, I don't think so.'

Tomas spoke hesitantly, groping for words, not always sure he was saying what he really thought. The English language was so different from Czech that it led him into uttering thoughts that would have lain below the surface back home. The presence of Charlotte led him on too. He was flattered that she had read these books at his prompting. He would have liked her to think he was more like Solzhenitzyn than he could have possibly been. It rankled that she had called him a puppet.

'I have a small present for you.' He had been sitting with the newspaper wrapped parcel on his knee and now he handed it over to her.

'A present? What is it?'

She unwrapped the parcel and found it contained a heart-shaped piece of glass with a coloured picture of Prague castle embedded in it. Turn the glass to one side and the picture changed. It now showed a river scene, the Vltava, with trees and boats. Turn it in the other direction and there was a picture of Wenceslas Square. Tomas explained all this with great pride, saying the present was of no great consequence but he had come across it by chance in the Portobello Road market and just had to buy it. These refracting glasses were made for the tourist trade. They were common so it was not surprising to find it where it was. The heart shape was meant to convey love for the city which indeed he had and although Charlotte had not been there he hoped she too might have a little of this love and one day go there.

'Why, it's just so cute. And so touching you should think of me when you bought it. Now what should I do with it? I'll put it in the bathroom so I'll see it every day. And Daniel will see it every day. When we go back to the States we'll put it in the bathroom there. Every time we see it we'll think of you. Have you ever thought of going to the States yourself? Your father talks of it.'

It amazed and slightly shocked Tomas that she should talk of Daniel as his father in this way. It was as though the knowledge he'd had this affaire all those years ago counted for nothing. Why was she not jealous? Why did she not reproach Daniel? Perhaps she did but there was no way of knowing from the light way she talked. In America they had such a different way of life, marrying and divorcing, moving from one place to another, from one job to another job, but always living in luxurious surroundings like the Blairs' flat here in London. Tomas knew all this from the American movies he had seen but he still could not understand why Charlotte should show such friendship for her husband's illegitimate son. She must love Daniel a great deal.

'I imagine you think it might be difficult for you to enter the States. Daniel doesn't think there'd be any difficulty. He has friends in the State Department who'd do him a favour. Anyway, you're a refugee from what our President is now calling the Evil Empire and that would help. It would also help if you had your birth certificate. Is that something that could be gotten hold of?'

Tomas would have expected Daniel to be happier with the width of the Atlantic between them, particularly as he would, as Charlotte had told him, be having an American son in the not so distant future.

No, he would not want to go to the States because that would mean cutting himself off from Prague even more completely; working in the Czech section of the BBC he felt in touch with his homeland. He knew more about what was going on there than he did when still in Prague. The Bush House canteen was where he heard a lot that did not find its way into the bulletins or news sheets, some of it just gossip, some of it guesswork that turned out to be not far off the truth, none of it hard enough to be reported but most of it pointing in the direction of momentous change. Whatever might be happening because of the Solidarity movement in Poland and Gorbachov's *glasnost* in the Soviet Union, Tomas had thought the regime was too firmly entrenched in Czechoslovakia for any change to be possible; the Husak regime was the most reactionary in Eastern Europe. But now he was not so sure, the ice might be melting even there. He tried to explain this to Charlotte.

'This is not a time for me to think of going to America.' He hesitated. 'You are so kind to me yet you of all people would have most cause to resent my existence.'

Charlotte laughed. 'No problem. Whatever pleases Daniel pleases me. No, perhaps that's not quite true,' she corrected herself, 'because I don't share all his tastes. That would be too much to expect. But his pleasure he takes in you is something I can share. If you ask me why he's so delighted I guess it's because it makes him feel a real helluva guy. But then he is, so why not let him behave that way?'

Delight in his existence! No one had ever said anything remotely like this to Tomas before and before he could restrain himself he had real tears in his eyes, they were running down his cheeks, and all he could do was search for his handkerchief and say, 'Excuse me, but I am not usually like this, I think I must go now.'

'I can't thank you enough for this lovely present.'

Still dabbing at his eyes. 'Its shape is a heart to show love for Prague. But when I saw it first I did not think of Prague, I thought of you.' And he rushed off.

He still did not know what to call her. He ought to call her simply Mrs Blair but was encouraged to call her Charlotte; this he felt would be an intolerable presumption. He could no more call her that than he could have called his own mother Vera. Having made a fool of himself by bursting into tears and made the embarrassing declaration he now assumed she would treat him more coolly; so out of his folly and lack of restraint might have come some good. It would be better for everyone if any future relationship was more arm-length.

In the Bush House canteen he was even more at home; whatever shyness and reserve he had now dropped away and he entered into conversations with a vigour and jokiness that Josh Smilan noticed and caused him to ask whether Tomas had found a girl friend.

'No, what would a girl want with me?'

'There are those who'd think you quite dishy, my boy. Have you never had a girl?'

Tomas thought Josh was asking whether he was a virgin and said he was, he had never made love and he tried not to think about girls in that way.

'Boys?'

'No, what are you saying? I've got enough longing for sex. I'm like anybody else. It's a discipline to be chaste and I like that kind of discipline.'

Josh told him he was quite right and he ought to write a book about it for the guidance of young people living in a world of sensuality and temptation.

'You're mocking me.'

'Sure I'm mocking you. You're different. Something has happened to you. If it isn't carnal delight what is it? Have you discovered your father was a rabbi?'

'Nothing has happened in the way you mean. I've dropped my Jewish dream. I've grown older all of a sudden.'

'How old are you in fact?'

'I don't mean older in years. I mean just – well, older!'

Lear was doing well at the Old Yard box office and Fred was in high good humour because he had negotiated a transfer to the Comedy Theatre in the West End which would provide the Old Yard with a goodly percentage rake-off and clear the theatre for a new play about local government corruption which had been on the stocks for a long time and was more in keeping with the Old Yard tradition than a revival of Shakespeare – profitable though that was and good for the company's morale to have won a West End transfer in a Shakespeare market usually cornered by the National and the Royal Shakespeare itself down at the Barbican.

In the warmth induced by so much achievement Fred learned that Tomas was coming up to a birthday and said they must mark the occasion with a few drinks in the Stalls bar. Tomas said he did not want celebratory drinks but if Fred wanted to know what would really please him it would be for the Old Yard company and the cast of

Lear to demonstrate outside the Czechoslovak Embassy with placards calling for the release of Karl Jacubek who was still in prison for having King Lear made up to look like Stalin.

'Why not?' said Fred. 'Lear calling to Lear across the frontiers. I like it. Good publicity too.'

The demonstration was not meant to rule out the drinks in the Stalls bar and Tomas was encouraged to invite his friends. Friends? Who were they, apart from the people he knew at the Old Yard? He could invite Josh Smilan and his wife. He could invite one of the editors from the Czech section at Bush House, and there was the secretary of Czech dissidents-in-exile group who specialised in smuggling *samizdat* literature. But could he invite Daniel and Charlotte? Mike the General Manager had been told by Fred to send out invitations and Tomas saw no harm in adding their names to the list. Once the cards had gone out he realised how desperately he wanted Charlotte to come. It would be unbearable if she failed to arrive.

The drinks were to be on a Tuesday, which was when the weekly script meeting was held, and after lunch. There was no knowing who would turn up because Mike had phrased the invitations casually – people were invited to 'drop in' and there was no R.S.V.P.; but being a Tuesday there would be lots of staff around so Tomas – Fred assured him – would have quite an audience for the few words that would be expected of him.

'By the way, how old will you be, Tomas?'

'Nineteen.'

'Jeez! Is that all? I had no idea,' said Fred. 'You don't look a day over twenty-one.'

The drinks being set for early afternoon nobody from the cast of *Lear* came; except for the day of the matinee they never showed up before six and Tomas was not affronted. But nearly all the others put in an appearance. Josh and his wife Leonie arrived with a parcel wrapped in green paper which Tomas was told not to open until he was alone. The people from the Czech section could not come because they were on duty but they had all signed a birthday card which Josh handed over on their behalf. Then Charlotte herself came in a transparent raincoat over a daffodil yellow costume with a red rose and maidenhair fern by way of corsage which she immediately presented to Tomas who stammered his thanks and kissed her gently on the cheek.

'Daniel is working. But the day is not over yet. There's quite a storm brewing. The sky's coming up like night. Just what King Lear ordered.'

She handed him a parcel which, like the one from Josh, was wrapped in green paper and the coincidence made Tomas wonder whether birthday parcels in England were, by tradition, always wrapped in green. Green for hope and new life. How very appropriate! He was nineteen and never before had he so sharply perceived the awareness of life's possibilities. He took a glass of the fizzy white wine – not champagne, that would have been too expensive – and drank it in one draught. Mike was immediately at his side to charge the glass afresh. Just anything could happen and all of it good and exciting – a life in the theatre, that is what he hoped for, perhaps as an actor, perhaps as a designer. For the first time in his life other people were on his side, even Mike the General Manager and Fred who had been hard on him in the past were almost cheering him on. Was it not the most fantastic good fortune that the theatre were giving him, a gauche stranger as he thought of himself, this marvellous party? What would they think of it at the Obelisk if only they knew? What would his mother think?

Fred proposed a toast, everybody drank and then Tomas was called on to say his few words. 'I have written a poem,' he said. 'It is a little lyric poem and it is in Czech, that goes without saying and I would read it but that would be a waste of time for you. I mean you would not understand. So let me say that it is about a bird. You know there are some birds that lose their way and arrive in countries where they are unknown. I am like one of those birds. That is what the poem says. So thank you for being so kind to a lost bird.'

'Bravo!' said Fred. 'Now we move on the Czech Embassy. The banners are stacked in the foyer. We'll go by the underground to Kensington High Street. Remember!' He clapped his hands to restore order and a little quiet because quite a lot of drinking and a babble of talk were still going on. 'Everybody back here by five o'clock at the latest, or there'll be trouble, I promise you.'

Once outside the theatre they could see an immense black cloud towering across the sun and rays of light breaking through gaps and at the edges. Lightning scissored down. Chimneys, roof tops and the tall finger of the Post Office tower were freaked in almost luminous black. The thunder shook the ground but as yet there was no rain. Tomas left his parcels in the office and was astonished to see Charlotte running with them to the underground.

'But you're not coming, are you?'

'Why not?' She waved an umbrella to show that she was ready for anything. At Kensington High Street they seemed to be at the centre of the storm. Rain cascaded from the guttering and downpipes, not big enough to cope. A clap of thunder was so violent immediately overhead and the dazzle of lightning that accompanied it left the air vibrating. The Old Yard crowd had to wait in the station until the worst of the rain had passed and then Fred insisted they pressed on to the Embassy or the Agency photographers he had alerted would assume they were not coming.

'We'll brave the storm. Think we are on Lear's heath. "And thou all-shaking thunder, smite flat the thick rotundity of the world." Where the hell's Julian? He promised to meet us here at three. I want a photo of our Lear holding a banner in the storm.'

Tomas caught Charlotte by the arm. 'You mustn't come.'

'I want to see what happens.' She was carrying one of the 'Release Karl Jacubek' banners. 'This storm will soon pass.'

'I beg you not to come out in the rain. I'll take your banner.' The thought of a pregnant Charlotte walking out in this rain made Tomas vehement. The most dreadful possibilities occurred to him. She might get soaked and catch a chill. Her baby might be harmed. She might be struck by lightning!

Charlotte had no such worries but by the time they reached the Embassy she was wet nevertheless. Neither her umbrella nor the transparent raincoat gave enough protection and her feet were soaked too. Julian was already there holding a huge red and white striped umbrella and they all posed for the press photographers, Fred holding an envelope which contained a letter to be handed in. Tomas and Charlotte struggled with their banner in the wind. It was so strong they had to fight to hold it aloft.

Because of the storm it was not an effective demonstration but they were all buoyed by the feeling it was Lear's storm they were battling against. Fred tried to get a chant going, 'Jacubek out!' After a word with the policeman on the gate he went to the front door and rang the bell. When it was opened the demonstrators cheered, Fred handed his letter over and that was that. The photographers drove off as Julian had to be helped to prevent his red and white umbrella being blown inside out by turning it into the wind. In the general retreat Tomas offered to get a cab for Charlotte but it was not far to the flat and she said she would rather walk.

'Daniel was sorry not to be at your party,' she said, 'but he'd love you to come round this evening. It doesn't matter how late.'

'Some other time,' he said. 'And thank you both for the present.'

'Wait till you open it.'

Over presents Tomas had always behaved oddly. He did not like them. Giving presents was a different matter; he liked to please and to give pleasure, so he had never failed to give his step-brothers small presents on their birthdays, and he had given Charlotte a present. But he himself did not want gifts, he told the boys and he told his mother too, without being able to give good reason for what she described as his lack of grace. It was just the same with the presents from Josh and Charlotte. He took the green parcels back to his bed-sitter and left them unopened for days.

When he unwrapped the first one it gave him quite a shock because it contained the heart-shaped piece of glass with the refracting coloured pictures of Prague. He looked at it incredulously. How could Charlotte be so brutal? Perhaps she had returned it on the instructions of Daniel but why, in that case, should they administer this stinging rebuff and at the same time make a fuss of him? The duplicity struck so hard he felt momentarily queasy. He looked inside the wrapping to see if there was a note that would explain their rejection of what he had innocently offered. Nothing. He dropped the glass in the hope it would shatter but it was tough and came to no harm. He stamped on it. He picked it up and beat at it with his clenched fist. A hammer would be needed to do any real damage and he had no hammer.

So that is what they really thought of him! It could only be contempt. He had been quite right to be wary of approaches from his so-called father. By giving way he had exposed himself to insult and his pride was so hurt he could, still feeling sick, only think of revenge. Daniel was jealous of him and his friendship with Charlotte. It was through this jealousy that he would try and hurt them and phrases suitable for putting into an abusive letter immediately surfaced. He would smash the Prague glass and send it back with a letter saying the fragments stood for their broken relationship. What you have done is spit in my face. You have shown a terrible, blank lovelessness and may your own marriage turn loveless too, as you deserve. For ever and ever and ever (Lear's 'never, never, never', at the back of his mind). You'll be followed by my hate.

At this point he opened the second parcel and found it contained a blue nylon raincoat with hood and drawstring so that it could be tightened under the chin. And here there was indeed a note. It said, 'We were so touched by your song about the wind and the rain we felt you really ought to have this protection. With love on your birthday, Charlotte and Daniel.'

Once he had understood his mistake Tomas's reaction was so strong he was unable to keep back the tears. On the other parcel, sure enough, there was a tie-on label from Josh and Leonie saying, 'We were unable to believe our luck in finding this magic glass from Prague and wanted to share our luck in the best way by giving it to you, Tomas, on your birthday.'

116

He could not think where they had found it. Perhaps in the same street market he had found one. There must be lots of them. He laughed and cried for quite some time and then put on the blue nylon raincoat to find it was a good fit. He pulled the hood over his head and tightened the cord so that, when he looked at himself in the mirror, he had a medieval look about, like a monk in his cowl all nose and teeth. It was like that, although it was a hot and sunny evening, he would go out and walk the pavements not caring what people thought of him in such a get-up; he would be just another of those oddities seen about London from time to time, talking loudly to himself and with tear-filled eyes.

On the night flight most of the passengers snoozed or watched a movie but Margaret talked to this rather agreeable man from Chicago who said he was joining a Swan Hellenic party in London and going on a Mediterranean cruise. She guessed he was about her age or a little older. He had a lot of white hair and a pink face but his manner was lively enough. His name was Edgar Bunce, a widower he said who had been in the insurance business all his life but he had retired early to enjoy himself. One son lived in California and sold computers, a daughter was a doctor and married to a doctor in Milwaukee.

'There comes a time when a man feels he's done as much for other people as he's capable of, so he begins to think of himself. I wasn't living for myself, I just lived through the kids. And my wife Tess was a great do-gooder. You know, money-raising for charity. It was fine, of course, she was a good woman. Without intending it, though, she made me feel stingy. I used to feel real guilty about that. But d'you know what? I don't feel guilty any more. Are you alone too?'

'I've a husband, if that's what you're asking. I'm going to see my daughter. She's pregnant but something seems to have gone wrong.'

'Uhu!'

'Couldn't have come at a worse time. I was organising the subscription concerts for our local orchestra. But I just had to drop everything.'

'That's tough.'

'There are other people in the team but if they know about selling tickets they don't know about music and vice versa. They relied on me. God knows what will happen. I was negotiating for some really top musician to come down and make a guest appearance.'

'What's local for you, Mrs – ?'

'Tampa. I'm Margaret Bentsen.'

'Philoprogenitive, that's the word I was trying to think of, Margaret. I like words, you know that? Loving one's kids. Yes, I've done my duty in that respect. And you obviously love your daughter.'

'It isn't as though we don't talk enough on the telephone. We're always calling each other but she seems to want to make a mystery of this pregnancy trouble.'

'I guess she just wants her mother around. So she married an Englishman, eh?'

'No, Daniel is in London on an assignment.'

Edgar said he was staying at the Stafford Hotel for a week or so before going off on his trip. He was going to look around town and take in a few shows and he would be really honoured if she allowed him to squire her around. London was a place a man could feel lonely in. Margaret sympathised but said she had no idea what demands Charlotte would be making and in any case her aim was to return to Tampa as soon as possible. She gave him Charlotte's address and telephone number. Edgar said a message left at the Stafford would always find him and when, the following morning, they parted at Heathrow it was with expressions of their mutual pleasure in one another's company.

She was met by Daniel at Heathrow and told him she had not a wink of sleep all night. This was the last time she took a night flight anywhere, even if it meant flying up to New York to make a connection. 'How's Charlotte?'

'She's O.K. She's just ordered to stay in bed.'

'For how long?'

'As long as it takes.' Len was on hand to carry Margaret's bags out to the car and drive them up the M4. 'I guess you must be exhausted, Margaret. We'll just drop you at the apartment. I'll go straight on to the office but you get to bed.'

'You mean that Charlotte's afraid of having a miscarriage?'

'That's about it. But I've gotten the finest gynaecologist in town and he says to feed her on smoked salmon and keep her immobile. Then there's a good chance of Alexander coming along as ordered.'

'Alexander?'

'Didn't Charlotte tell you? We know it's a boy and that's what we've called him, Alexander.'

'My friend Ruth Schneider's daughter had a long lie-in like that and had a lovely boy.'

'It's so boring for her, lying there day after day, week after week. And do you know what, she doesn't object to the nurse coming in every morning and there's a woman who does the cleaning and a bit of cooking. But Charlotte insists I grill her the salmon steaks myself. I wanted her to

121

have them sent over from Harrods but she said no, she wanted them fresh grilled and she wanted me to do it myself. What's so special about grilled salmon anyway?'

'What started this off? Charlotte been playing tennis?'

'No, she won't admit this but I suspect it all started when she went out on that demonstration in a storm and got herself soaked.'

'What demonstration?'

'At the Czech embassy. It was a protest against some theatre director in Prague being locked up.'

'Why should Charlotte get mixed up in a thing like that?'

'Surely Charlotte has told you about Tomas? He's the Czech son I knew nothing about.'

No, Charlotte had not told her about Tomas and when Daniel explained she was so dismayed she stared unbelievingly out of the car window at the office blocks, the factories and the tiny houses – how tiny everything was in England, and how dirty! – that slowly slid past. It was untrue that she had not slept a wink but she was tired nevertheless and could have done without this information that Daniel was giving her – and with such enthusiasm! Didn't he understand the significance of what he was saying? Charlotte had an illegitimate stepson and that realisation alone might have been enough to bring on a miscarriage, irrespective of any storm. And here was Daniel talking about his bastard as though it was nothing to be ashamed of.

'You've been imposed on,' she said at last. 'You knew nothing of this boy's existence until he turned up in England. The woman is blackmailing you.'

'It's not like that at all, Margaret. You'll see for yourself when you meet him.'

'I have no wish whatsoever to meet him, Daniel, and I'm surprised you should even suggest it.'

Daniel took her bags up to the apartment and then went straight on to the office as promised so Margaret did not have the opportunity of telling him, in Charlotte's presence, how much he had shocked her. That would come later. In the meantime, there was Charlotte in bed, looking surprisingly radiant in a bed-jacket embellished with what looked like Van Gogh sunflowers, a huge TV set on a stand at the foot of her bed. The poor girl was obviously delighted to see her. What she must have gone through! To have evidence of a former amour sprung on her by Daniel would have been bad at the best of times, but when pregnant it was intolerable. She could not, as no doubt she would have liked, just throw Daniel out. She was held hostage by Daniel's unborn child. But throw Daniel out was what it would eventually come to and Margaret was already determined to do what lay in her power to bring this about. One of Simon's Sci-fi stories was set at some time in the future when women had control of a sperm bank and were independent of men if they so chose. That was how it should be.

Margaret bent over to kiss and hug Charlotte, saying, 'Darling, I just had to come. No, tell me, just what is wrong?'

'The baby has moved.'

'Moved?'

'It's O.K. but he's moved. This has put a strain on some stalk, I can't remember its name, but all will be well if I take it easy. Can you imagine it? Could be a couple of months.'

Margaret wondered why she had come. There was no question of her hanging around for a couple of months. She went straight off to the spare bedroom thinking

Charlotte could have spared her the inconvenience of the trip if she had been more forthcoming on the telephone about what was wrong with her pregnancy. Perhaps it was not so simple. Perhaps that nice travelling companion of hers, Edgar Bunce, was right and the girl just wanted her mother around. The important next step would be to see the gynaecologist and check whether Charlotte was fit enough to be flown back to the States.

Margaret studied herself in the dressing table mirror. Tired as she was the impression nevertheless was reassuring. Thank God she had never had to worry about her weight. He had blessed her with a metabolism that kept her naturally around 140 pounds. Someone had told her she bore a strong resemblance to Mrs Robinson as portrayed by Gainsborough in the role of Perdita. When she saw a reproduction of the painting she accepted the likeness – the same beautiful fair hair, the same delicate oval face and firm chin, though the set of the mouth was not quite right; lips too compressed as though in indignation and the light hazel eyes too cold. Mrs Robinson looked a bitch, to be honest, but if the expression was softened and the eyes made larger an undoubted resemblance would emerge. Margaret thought she made a genial impression on people – Edgar Bunce had certainly thought so – and once she'd been able to spend a couple of hours at the hairdresser's the effects of the night flight would be cleared up and her normal radiance restored.

By lunchtime she was sufficiently revived to eat the omelette that the daily prepared for her and Charlotte, so much so she was able to go into the worrying matter of the supposed Czech son. She was not entirely surprised to learn that Daniel had a guilty secret; she had never warmed to the man. He had remained a bachelor until (what was it?) over thirty-five so there must have been something the matter with him; he was either a homosexual or a womaniser, neither of which Margaret could stand. What was more he talked too much and had the hide of an Everglades alligator. Charlotte needed a spell away from him and the sooner the better, the pregnancy notwithstanding, so that she could make up her mind what sort of future they had together.

'Why didn't you tell me about this boy?' Margaret demanded.

To her astonishment Charlotte did not consider the existence of Tomas to be worrying at all. 'It all happened so long ago.'

'But this woman, his mother, might arrive at any moment and then where would you be?'

'No chance of that. Daniel says he can't even remember what she looks like and in any case she's married with two other sons. It's all ancient history, Meg.'

'Nothing in anybody's past is ancient history. It's all there and alive until the day you die.'

What was she thinking to make her say that? Perhaps nothing more than what was brought on by being in England again in spite of all she had done to keep out of the place. Those sodden clouds and of all those houses with chimneys on them had stirred memories she would rather do without.

One of the remarks made by Edgar on that night flight stayed with her, the one about not living for himself but just living through the kids. She knew the feeling. A lot of nervous energy had been spent empathising with Charlotte, but nothing compared with the outpouring she had undergone – and resented – from her own father. As a one-time Guards officer he wanted her to achieve something comparable. She had to be shoved up the ladder of success; and that meant, first and foremost, getting her into Oxford and not into the kind of red-brick university where he failed to win as good a degree in mathematics and physics as he had expected. This meant going through old maths scholarship papers with her every Saturday morning and, sure enough, she did win a place at Somerville. When the news came through he said it was the greatest day of his life. But he said exactly the same some years later when she married Owen Bark by special licence from the bishop in the chapel of St Ebbe's College. In the face of opposition from Mummy, and a little opposition from Margaret herself, he pulled strings, lobbied, bent his prospective son-in-law's ear, and brought off this triumphant wedding in the venerable setting wherein, if there was any justice in the world, his own formative years would have been spent.

He wore a silver grey top hat and morning suit. He displayed his war medals even though he had been told they should not be properly worn on such a suit. No opportunity for display was to be missed on this second great day when his daughter became doubly Oxonian, a graduate in her own right and as the wife of a university lecturer. It was a moment when he wanted everyone to know by the digit on his Africa Star he had served with the Eighth Army. It turned out there was to be no other such moment. She was an only child so there was nobody else to coach in maths and provide more vicarious achievement. He left Margaret with the feeling she had been manipulated to serve his own self-importance.

Daniel had mastered micro-wave cooking and could serve up in no time at all excellent salmon steaks with asparagus, croquette potatoes and mayonnaise sauce. One evening he even managed a lemon soufflé. Cooking gave him pleasure. Taking a cordon bleu cookery course would be the most fantastic way of spending a holiday, he said, provided it was in Bayreuth, say, when he could attend performances of the Ring cycle in the evening. If some day the bottom dropped out of fund managing he could start a classy restaurant somewhere in up-state New York where patrons could drop in by helicopter; in time Alexander would take over and become the most famous chef in America. If there was any dish Meg specially fancied he was at her service: *boeuf Stroganoff*, for example, or *steak en croute*. With the salmon he served what he described as a nippy Sancerre which would do no harm to anyone and followed this with a chocolate icecream *bombe* from Harrod's food store. Charlotte would not take even a single glass of wine but Alexander must otherwise be acquiring a taste in good fare that would set him up for life.

Margaret was forced to agree Daniel had his good points. When Edgar Bunce called to take her out to her first dinner date Margaret introduced him by saying, while he was still coming up in the lift, that she felt sorry for him because he was all alone in London. He took her to a Greek restaurant in Soho and they talked of his Mediterranean trip. Why did she not come along? From what he had seen Charlotte did not need any help Margaret could give and she was well looked after by her husband, so why not live for herself just for a change? There came a point when you just had to start treating family like any other people.

'Charlotte and I are very close,' said Margaret.

'My experience is it doesn't pay to be too close.'

'Simon would go nuts. He's the jealous type.'

She had already told him about the Czech boy and Edgar had plainly been turning the information over in his mind. 'All you need to tell Simon is that you need to get over the shock. Now, don't tell me. It must have been a shock to discover Daniel had this in his past. And

somebody coming from a commie state like Czechoslovakia, too! So you had this shock, O.K.? And you need a
break to get over it.'

'Out of the question, Edgar. I haven't given up hope of
taking Charlotte back home with me.'

'Think it over. The tour group doesn't leave for another
week and I've checked there are vacancies. Be my guest.'

The suggestion excited her so much she let Edgar kiss
her on the mouth when he dropped her at the entrance to
the Blairs' apartment block and she went up to join
Charlotte and Daniel in such a flutter she had to go
straight to her room to compose herself.

'Will it be O.K. if I ring Simon?' She had carefully
dabbed round her eyes, walked back into the living room
and called into the Blairs' bedroom. They were both
intent on a TV programme. Charlotte told her to go
ahead, using the phone in her own room so that she would
not be bothered by the TV. It would be early evening in
Tampa.

Margaret knew what Simon would be doing. He would
have changed out of his swim suit and put on slacks and
one of his floral shirts, so covering his unusually hairy
chest, to sit by the pool with a tall bourbon on the rocks.
He would have his notebook handy in case he wanted to
jot down whatever occurred to him but most of the time
he did nothing, he just gazed with half-shut eyes into the
little grove of dwarf palm. He would have to get up when
the phone rang and walk back into the house, limping
because of the old stiffness in his right knee. She would
have to be patient. After she heard the broken purr that
signalled she had got through she would have to wait.

'Hiya, it's me,' she said when she heard the familiar
grunt. 'You'll have forgotten about me, darling, but I've
not forgotten you. Sure, I'm O.K. Charlotte's just laid

up, you know. It's a matter of staying in bed in case she precipitates a miscarriage. Yeah, that's the awful possibility but the gynaecologist says not to worry, there's a good chance that everything will be O.K. D'you know what? They know it's to be a boy and they've decided to call him Alexander. But look, Simon. You're coping all right? Things are so quiet here I thought I might pop over to Paris for a few days and do some shopping. Or Milan. Yes, a wardrobe replenishment. What's the weather like with you? Raining here. It always seems to be raining. Charlotte was caught in a rainstorm and Daniel reckons that might have started the trouble.'

And now he would go straight back to that bourbon on the rocks and, after a while, start tapping away at his word processor because all the time she had been talking he had, she knew, been thinking of some new quirk in his Sci-Fi saga. It would have been kinder to Simon if she had been able to take more interest in it. But space travel, hairy hominids and robots, didn't grab her; she liked her fiction populated by men and women like herself, intelligent and attractive people who led interesting lives of a kind she would like to lead herself. She ought to have been a novelist. The important part of her life had been not in the boring happenings of everyday life but in the imagination. She had not exploited herself. That was the truth of the matter. She had devoted too much of herself to other people, to Simon and Charlotte when she ought to have cultivated herself. Hadn't that nice Edgar said something of the sort?

She slept late and when she went into the kitchen to make herself coffee and toast found Mrs Tracey, the daily, already there which meant it must be past ten.

'The vicar's come,' said Mrs Tracey.

'The vicar?'

129

'He comes regular, does the vicar.'

Margaret took a bath and dressed slowly. When she eventually emerged the vicar was still there, sitting on a chair at Charlotte's bedside but preparing to go because he stood up and smiled broadly as she entered. He was bespectacled, owlish and plump. Margaret was surprised to see him because although she well-knew from her previous marriage that visiting the sick was an important part of an Anglican priest's duties she had no idea Charlotte would encourage it.

Charlotte introduced her. 'My mother. This is Michael Bellamy.'

He shook her by the hand, saying, 'It is a privilege to meet you, Mrs Bark. Your husband is well known to us all in our part of the church because, of course, his articles in *The Courier* are written from an Anglo-Catholic point of view, and with such warmth. I have often meant to write to him. Will you please say how much his articles are appreciated? Can't he be persuaded to write more frequently? Once a month is really not enough for such wisdom.'

The silence disconcerted him.

'I ought to have explained,' said Charlotte, 'that my mother was Mrs Bark but she hasn't been that for many years. Sorry, Meg.'

'I'm sorry too,' said the priest. 'Have I been very clumsy?'

'Yes, but unwittingly. I'm Mrs Bentsen now.'

The implications immediately caused the Reverend Michael Bellamy to blush girlishly and wave his arms about. Not Mrs Bark! he was obviously thinking. Then Owen Bark must have had a divorce and that was not in accord with the Catholic position he stood for. Was it possible there was some dreadful inconsistency? It would be more than an inconsistency; it would be a scandal!

Margaret, aware of what was going through the man's mind, was determined not to help in the slightest and reserved her anger for Charlotte who really should not have exposed her in this way.

'I think I'll leave you to whatever you were talking about,' she said.

'Please, Mrs – er, I was on the point of leaving myself.'

'Mr Bellamy is preparing me for confirmation, Meg. Why did you never have me confirmed?'

Never have her confirmed? Coming from Charlotte this was a strange question when she knew they had not been to a religious service in years, unless funerals and weddings were counted. Simon was a non-believer, she was a non-believer and she had always been a non-believer even when she was married to Owen and outwardly conformed to the practices he thought necessary, the weekly eucharist mainly, while remaining inwardly indifferent. Whatever put confirmation into Charlotte's head? Or who put it there? Owen? Was it through contact with her father?

After the Reverend Michael Bellamy had gone Charlotte repeated her question and Margaret said confirmation did not form part of their life style. Some of their friends and acquaintances went to services of one kind or another but it was more a social thing, as Charlotte well knew. Most did not go to services. In any case, confirmation was up to the individual. No, that was not being honest. In the face of family indifference Charlotte would have needed to be unusually pious to offer herself for confirmation and she was more interested in such worldly matters as dating and getting good grades. Margaret's indifference had deep roots. She just could not understand how the crucifying of a man no matter how good two thousand years ago could in any sense save her. She had tried and failed. She read various Christian apologetics and was baffled even to know what being saved meant and was repelled by the imagery – being washed by the blood of the Lamb, and so on. Owen was quite unaware of her disbelief and she could not be bothered to enlighten him.

'Is this something your father has talked you into?'

'No. I just felt like it, that's all.'

Margaret thought it best to be brisk and commonsensical. 'It's no business of mine. If that's the way you want it.'

'I guess I had an experience.' It was one of those days when Charlotte dressed and walked up and down in her bedroom for exercise. Her local GP was expected to look in at any moment to take her blood pressure and report on some tests so, as she said, what with religious instruction, sympathetic chat from the doctor and *The Times* crossword to which she had become addicted, life was just one whirl of activity.

'What sort of an experience?'

'Hard to say. I was going past a church and went in. Lit a candle. Perhaps it's just being pregnant but I suddenly felt there was more of me. Not just Alexander.'

'What does Daniel think?'

'He's all in favour. But then the way I am he'd be in favour of anything I wanted to do. I'm sorry about the Mrs Bark bit. It seemed natural to tell Michael my father was in orders too and it was a bit of a surprise he'd even heard of him. I didn't know father wrote for a paper. Michael showed me some cuttings and I thought they were interesting.'

'I shall go out and do some shopping. Is there anything I can get you?'

'Strange, isn't it, that father still thinks of you as Mrs Bark?'

Pregnancy took women in different ways. When she was having Charlotte she took to eating bits of coal. It was an irrational craving that left her with a black tongue and lips she had to clean up after every snack. She was friendly with a South African woman at the time who was also pregnant and she sent to Johannesburg for green monkey flesh, whatever that was. Perhaps Charlotte's religious enthusiasm came into the same category. Strange appetites and longings could disappear as unexpectedly as they came. But it was mortifying that no sooner had she set foot in England out of motherly and entirely praise-worthy concern for Charlotte's welfare than the wretched Owen makes his presence felt, through the person of that bespectacled little priest, Michael what's-his-name, and the cuttings he so tiresomely had produced. If Charlotte so much as suggested she read them she, already angry over the Mrs Bark accusation (for so she felt it) would let fly.

'Don't expect me back for lunch. I'll have a bite out somewhere.'

So that is what he had told her, that he still thought of her as his wife. What other poison had Owen injected? In Kensington High Street she called a cab and asked to be taken to the Stafford Hotel in the hope of seeing Edgar but of course he was not there at that time of day. No, she would not leave a message. Trafalgar Square was within easy walking distance so she decided to calm herself by going to see Gainsborough's portrait of Mrs Robinson in the National Gallery. London was bright and cheerful. Beyond the Duke of York's statue she could see the full green of the trees in the Mall. Red double deckers popped up as in travel posters. Tourists, the usual nuisance, were everywhere but then wasn't she a tourist herself? Not quite. She knew this country. She knew these people in a way, even now, she did not know the mainly hispanic Americans she was living among. And she was not carrying a camera, was not a member of any group, she was alone and walking to see an old ghost who was still haunting her so she could not possibly be a tourist, could she?

Looking for the Gainsborough was tiring and she broke off to queue for coffee. She had been to the galleries showing British 18th century painting and the Gainsborough was not there. Perhaps her memory had played a trick and the painting was not in the National Gallery at all. Nobody to ask. The people selling postcards would not know, it would be too much to expect any of the attendants, so she drank her coffee and summoned the ghost up out of her own memory. What did Mrs Robinson as Perdita have to say to her 20th century incarnation?

If Edgar had been at the Stafford when she called she would have accepted his invitation to go on that Mediterranean trip but since then the walk in the sunshine, threading her way through the tourists, had sobered her. It was not like her. It was not like her to act so impulsively, that is what Mrs Robinson said; and always be truthful and candid. She always had been, hadn't she? She had never said one thing and done another. Some – her mother, in particular – had said her blunt way of talking was ill-bred but, for God's sake! what did breeding count for nowadays? Never do anything underhand and always speak her mind, that had been her way and she was not going to change now whatever the consequences. Silly old Owen, who even now was lurking in her background – or Charlotte's background, rather – could have testified she dealt openly and honestly with him.

Owen, as she now remembered, was the one who had told her of her resemblance to Mrs Robinson and taken her to see the portrait where she realised it was, not in the National Gallery but in the Wallace Collection way back up behind Oxford Street. When she saw it she had not been flattered. But she had bought a postcard-sized reproduction and stuck it up on the mirror of her dressing table where it grew on her and yes, she became increasingly sympathetic to this 18th century actress with her own colouring and a haughty attitude that could be imitated. Owen thought Mrs Robinson looked sweet but that only showed how little feeling he had for art; she was anything but sweet and Margaret was not going to be sweet either.

When she started her affair with Simon she told Owen without being able to say what it would lead to and Owen, after being very upset, had hoped it would not lead anywhere, for Charlotte's sake if not for his own. He had been almost comically dignified. The counter-measures he proposed – going on holiday, buying a motor-car (that was something they were without) or a television set (another lack) – were absurd and inadequate. Owen had what he described as a man-to-man talk with Simon. This naturally distressed him, but what did he expect? The point was that she had been perfectly open with Owen. She would be open now.

That meant talking to Simon and to Charlotte too. Cabs were discharging visitors to the Gallery outside so she was able to get away smartly in one of them only to be confronted, as soon as they turned out of Kensington High Street, with a police car and ambulance both flashing lights and policemen running white tapes across the street to keep out the crowd.

'Bomb scare,' said the cabbie. 'I'll have to drop you here, lady.'

135

Margaret approached one of the policemen and said, 'I've got to get in there. My daughter's in the apartment two floors over the entrance and she's confined to her bed.'

'We're clearing the flats now. There's no question of anyone going in. Sorry! I understand your feelings but there's probably a bomb under that parked car.'

'Who'd be crazy enough to plant a bomb there? This is just an ordinary residential area.'

'We're coping as quickly as we can, madam, but my instructions are not to let anyone past this tape.'

For the first time she was seeing for herself how people coped with a bomb scare. They were jostling to get a better view of the parked car which was being scrutinised at a distance by two policemen in flat caps, one of them using his walkie-talkie.

'Get back! Everyone back!' Helmeted police stretched out their arms. A man in khaki overalls and a medieval-looking head protection, a visor that pulled down over his face, ducked under the tape and made for the car carrying a large black case. Margaret could see people coming out of the entrance to Charlotte's block and being ushered along the pavement but there was no sign of Charlotte. She calculated that by ducking under the tape like that man with the black case she could get past the first line of police but these other men clearing the building would be more difficult. She wondered whether being hysterical and screaming would be any help.

She pushed at the nearest policeman. 'If my daughter's in there when this thing goes off I want to be with her.'

Someone touched her on the arm and she turned to find a young man in a zip-up jacket and jeans lowering his head to talk in her ear.

'They'll never let you through,' he said, 'but I think I

know how to get round behind the building into the next little street. There must be another way out.'

He had an alert, concerned expression on his face that conveyed more clearly than words, 'I understand how you feel and it is my wish to help.' Perhaps it was the big dark eyes that gave her the greatest reassurance. They were doggy-like – extraordinary to remember something so irrelevant at such a time – but remember she did, the eyes of Ruby the dachshund bitch who had kept her company for half the time they spent in Pittsburgh and was so loved even the thought of replacing her when the time came was too disloyal to contemplate. It was Ruby who stopped her brushing off this young man for his presumption. 'I heard what you said about your daughter.'

Even when he took her by the arm she did not shake him off; she was able to think of only one thing, Charlotte's safety. God knows what the shock of an explosion just outside her flat would do to the baby. But the girl was obstinate and might refuse to move. Margaret could just imagine that obstinacy. Being carried into the back bedroom would be about as much as she would allow but unless Margaret was there to supervise the move might be clumsily done. What else could you expect from policemen? Margaret had decided to make one more appeal to be allowed through when there was a flurry of excitement around the parked car. Men were backing away. Some had thrown themselves on the ground.

'Please let me guide you,' said the youth with the doggy eyes. As he seemed to know what to do and she did not she allowed herself to be led through the crowd back down the street and round the corner into a mews that gave access to an alley where there were dustbins, an old mattress and a bicycle with a front wheel missing. But there were a couple of policemen here too. They were

137

preventing people entering the flats from the rear and ushering away those who had come down the ironwork fire-escapes.

Margaret screamed. 'There she is!'

A couple of ambulance men were struggling with a stretcher on one of the fire-escapes. This time she was able to brush aside the restraining arm of a policeman and rush into a yard where there were more dustbins, followed by the youth who had guided her to Charlotte. Yes, it was most definitely Charlotte on that stretcher. Margaret could see her clearly. She was waving an arm because the stretcher was now so angled she could look down into the yard.

'How on earth did you find your way round here Meg?' she asked some minutes later. 'What fun this all is! Though what the IRA have against me I can't imagine.'

'You're all right, Charlotte? You really are safe and all right?'

'Sure I'm all right. But I'll be more all right when I've been able to talk to Daniel and tell him in person that I'm all right.'

'Best thing is to take you round to Casualty, ma'am,' said one of the ambulance men and they would have walked off with her.

'Thank you so much young man,' Margaret said and impulsively kissed the young man on the cheek.

'Hallo, Tomas.' Charlotte had at last caught sight of him. 'I'm glad you two have gotten acquainted.'

'Tomas?' Margaret looked at the young man more sharply. Giving him that peck on the cheek had been impulsive but it might turn out to be a peck she would like to cancel.

'Daniel's son.' Charlotte was being carried to the ambulance, Margaret walking at her side. 'You'll have to call

Daniel at the office, Meg. Emphasise everything's O.K.
I'm O.K. Alexander's O.K. You'll do that straight away,
won't you? The number? Christ! I don't carry that sort of
information in my head, what do you think? Look it up
in the book. Tomas will look it up for you. The Wheatley-
Minotaur Group.'

Tomas was speaking in Margaret's ear with the detest-
able familiarity he had used before. 'From what you were
saying about a daughter in that apartment I knew you just
had to be Charlotte's mother.'

His foreign accent was, to her ears, unpleasantly more
obvious and she decided to ignore him. She was determined to accompany Charlotte in the ambulance and
equally determined that Tomas should not. She did not
have the pleasure of barring his way because he made no
move towards the ambulance. This was the moment when
on the other side of the line of buildings the bomb went
off and the ground under their feet punched upwards. The
sound of the explosion was choked off as though the
sound track of a movie was cut to make way for a different
reverberation, the grumble of retreating thunder. The
shattering and tinkling of broken glass came in a cascade.
Smoke rose in a great whoosh. Charlotte had already been
placed in the ambulance and Margaret, after a brief
argument with one of the ambulance men, stepped in to
sit opposite with the satisfaction of knowing that cheeky
Czech boy had been left behind.

Charlotte said she was all right but then she would,
wouldn't she? There was no knowing what harm had
been done. Margaret wanted the ambulance men to take
her to the private clinic Charlotte was used to but they
said their drill was to take her to the nearest hospital. The
quicker the better. They had to get back to the site of the
explosion. Margaret was angry with them but her real

rage was for the way she had been caught up in this intolerable act of terrorism. What had she ever done to be treated in this way? Her reluctance ever to come to England had been horribly justified. Fate was against her. It might even force her to abandon that delightful Mediterannean cruise. How could she go off with a clear conscience when Charlotte and Daniel's flat had just been wrecked and they would have all the hassle of relocating? Just at the moment she had made up her mind to go on this spree, and to tell Simon and Charlotte about it, she was plunged into a crisis of conscience. On the one hand, motherly instincts and duty; on the other something more positive, a way of saying yes to life. It was quite infuriating to be pulled up short in this idiotic way.

In Casualty Reception Charlotte was transferred to a stretcher on wheels and trundled away while Margaret found a pay-phone and a pile of directories which did not list any Wheatley-Minotaur Group and she had to call Enquiries. By the time she was given a number a couple of stretcher cases went past the kiosk, one man with a great bloodstained pad on the side of his face and the other, a policeman, holding his helmet and chatting with his orderly; the first in from the bombing, she assumed.

'I'm sorry but Mr Blair is in a meeting,' said the secretary at the other end of the line with the usual English whine, made in part from a desire to ingratiate but also, so Margaret diagnosed, sinus trouble. When she said Mr Blair must be pulled out of that meeting the girl said it was a really important meeting and she had instructions not to interrupt. Eventually Margaret persuaded her to take in a note that said, 'Your wife is all right but she had to be moved out of the flat because of a bomb. She is in the Fulham South Hospital.' Having written this down the girl said 'Oh dear!' and that she was sure it would be O.K. to take the note in.

She also called the Stafford in the hope of speaking to Edgar Bunce but he must have been out because there was no reply from his room, so she left a message saying her daughter's flat had been bombed. She and Charlotte were unscathed but she did not know what had happened to the police and the members of the bomb disposal unit. The reception clerk at the Stafford was able to help her here because he had been listening to the radio. Only minor casualties, he said, but buildings had been shattered. When she reported back to Charlotte she saw the girl had been crying. It was delayed shock, no doubt, and that meant she must be got away from this awful place, into some decent hotel and her pet gynaecologist whistled over from the Clinic.

'We must wait for Daniel,' said Charlotte.

At this moment Tomas walked in, seized one of Charlotte's hands and kissed it. 'It's not so bad. I've been round to look at the damage. The police wouldn't let me near because there's a big gas leak and they're afraid of an explosion. The water main is broken so there's flooding. But I could see from a distance. All the windows of all the houses are gone. But the houses themselves are standing up. I think a soldier was killed because the bomb went off before they expected. So I made it my business to find out where you'd been taken. Here I am to do what I can to help.'

Charlotte was still tremulous. 'What do you think has happened to all my clothes? I haven't brought a thing.'

By the time Daniel arrived – it must have been a good two hours later – Charlotte had been seen by a couple of doctors and, in spite of Margaret's protests, taken up three floors to a general ward where as her immediate neigh-

141

bours she had a West Indian woman and a gaunt lady who had a crucifix over her bed and a large bowl of fruit at her side which she immediately offered not only to Charlotte but to Margaret as well. Through the window there was a view of the river, three barges going upstream in tow and the tall chimneys of Battersea Power station on the other side presented like great guns against the heavens. Daniel was furious at the time Len had taken to drive him there. Not his fault. Just the traffic, worst of all in Kensington because of this bomb. He sat at Charlotte's bedside describing the traffic. He was glad to know Tomas had been around and made himself useful.

'He would have gone to salvage some of our stuff,' said Charlotte. 'The police wouldn't let him through. He was on duty at Bush House too. So he went off. He was marvellous. Meg was marvellous too, weren't you dear?'

'No, let's face it. I'm just all churned up. I'm that angry I just can't tell you. Why should these bombers pick on us?'

Daniel said he'd been listening on the car radio where it was reported some VIP in the Intelligence Service lived three doors up and the attack had been directed against him. The bomb had been stuck under his car though God knew how the bombers had managed it. They probably knew this guy could get away with parking on double yellow lines. He went off to find one of the doctors who had examined Charlotte and came back to say, 'It's O.K. to move you out of here. The Brownings said we can move in with them which is real nice, isn't it? But I don't like getting too cozy with business associates, I'd rather be independent. I asked Len to drive over to the Royal Garden and see whether they had rooms they could let us have. You'll come with us, of course, Meg. Of course it will be all right. We couldn't do without you.'

Margaret was on the point of saying she would not need to accept this hospitality because she was leaving for her Mediterranean cruise with Edgar Bunce any day now when she realised she would be doing nothing of the sort. She had already decided where her duty lay and, smouldering with rage though she was, could see no decent way of avoiding it. No knowing whether her clothes could be salvaged from the flat anyway. Everything would be shot through with glass splinters and fouled up with gas fumes and the water firemen loved splashing around at the least encouragement. She could imagine it all. Charlotte looked too pale to have come out of this bombing unscathed so, yes, she would move into the Royal Garden with them though at this time of year they might not have vacancies.

There followed a period of hanging about and great uncertainty because Len took an unconscionable time reporting back from the Royal Garden. Margaret said she could not sit about twiddling her thumbs. She'd find a taxi and go back to the flat on the chance she'd be allowed in to salvage what she could. First of all Daniel wanted to come with her, then he decided his place was with Charlotte; she had never seen him in such a dither. Would it be best if he stayed up here in the ward or should he go down to Casualty Reception because that would be where Len would show up? Margaret left him arguing with Charlotte. No, she did not know what she would do if the police turned her away. Something wild and get herself arrested probably.

But she was not turned away. The water main had been shut off, the gas fracture plugged and workmen had arrived in the Royal Borough of Kensington and Chelsea vans to sweep up broken glass. No, it was not true a soldier had been killed. A breakdown truck was being backed up to the shattered car which had taken the force of the bomb. Just there some of the brick facade of the block had collapsed into the road. The Blairs' flat appeared to have lost its windows but the entrance seemed more or less intact and Margaret was making for it, together with a couple of other people from the same block, when a police superintendent stopped them. He wanted to be sure they were bona fide residents.

'You think we might be looters?' Margaret decided more was to be gained by keeping her temper than telling the superintendent what she thought of him.

'I just want to be sure you're bona fide. Just collect what is absolutely necessary, then these flats will be sealed. I give you half an hour. Then I've got men coming in to board up the windows and make the doors secure. I'm sorry but that's the way it is.'

Margaret had her own key to let her into the flat. The windows were just holes in the wall with a gritty wind blowing through them. Daniel's leather armchair of which he was so proud was up-ended, the settee which had backed on to the windows had been thrown forward. She could not take a step without treading on glass. There was a nasty smell. Scorched brick? Burning cloth? Whisky? A broken whisky bottle explained that. The village where she lived as a child had a cottage industry of basket making and the acrid smell of the flat reminded her of osier boiling. The withies were stewed in vats and gave off a stink that made her feel sick whenever she caught a whiff. This smell was not that bad but it was bad enough to make her, momentarily, that child again; and as confused as that child would be in the shattered flat; so shattered it was like being in the street itself, talk coming up from the police and those other men in uniform. She did not know who they were. The windows gone, those men might have been up there with her, talking about the wrecked car. 'You can't lift it,' one of them said. 'It would disintegrate. We've got to shovel it up.'

The telephone rang. The sound was so unexpected she screamed. No electricity, no gas, but the telephone system still operated and she thought this remarkable. But where was the receiver? It went on ringing and eventually she located it under Daniel's upturned chair. Probably it would be Daniel himself because it would be just like him to assume telephones still worked in chaos. But the man's voice she heard after she had lifted the receiver and said hallo was certainly not Daniel's; it was thinner, higher pitched and obviously English.

'Shah! Is that you Shah? Oh, thank God. Say you're all right?'

'Yes, I'm all right,' she said. She was quite accustomed to being mistaken for Charlotte on the telephone. Their voices were remarkably alike, she had been told, and it would not be the first time she kept up the pretence just for the hell of seeing where it would take her.

'First of all we heard the news on the radio. Then your Aunt Eleanor telephoned to say she had seen the television news and she was sure the outrage was where you lived. Is that so, Shah? And is Daniel all right? But you are the main object of concern. Do you mean your flat isn't damaged at all? Eleanor said she had seen a number on the door of one of the houses and it was only four away from yours. She telephoned Scotland Yard. It just didn't occur to her you could be reached on the telephone. Thank God I'm so stupid I did not understand how unlikely it would be your phone was still working. That's what your aunt Eleanor told me. But it is! And I'm talking to you! Oh, thank God! Thank God!'

'The flat is wrecked.' After a quarter of a century or

more she was talking to Owen once more and she was more affected than she would have thought possible. Undeniably there was a tiny shock of pleasure. But she was being challenged, that was the main feeling, and she just had to defy that challenge. As always Owen sounded pompous which even he must have found difficult in the circumstances. He called the bombing an outrage. Well, it was but outrage seemed the sort of word that came up in official statements. Why didn't he just say it was terrible? She remembered Eleanor well enough and could relish the way she told Owen he was stupid to think the phone would be working. His voice was an old man's, a bit shaky. Even all those years ago it had not been really strong. When he had to pitch it up to make the invocations in the college chapel the strain made him sound quite emotional. 'Lift up your hearts,' he would cry, his voice breaking, 'Let us give thanks unto our Lord God.' Such exertions would be beyond him now.

'The fact that you are there and all right is enough for me, Shah. I have been praying. It all makes me feel humble. Are you lying in bed? That is how I have imagined you all this time. Doesn't that mean you were there when this bomb went off?'

'No, I was away in time. This place is uninhabitable. We're going to check into a hotel and that's what Daniel is fixing this very minute.'

'That's very wise.'

'You'll be glad to know my mother is with us. She's been quite wonderful as you'd expect. She's a great support.'

'Your mother?' After some moments of silence. 'That is very good news. How very fortunate. For a moment I thought she might have come because of the bomb. But

146

of course there would not have been time. She's been with
you for a while?'

'Ten days.'

'Is she unaccompanied?'

'Simon is not with her, if that's what you're asking.'

She could tell by the silences and the odd gasps that he
had been nonplussed to learn that she, Margaret, was in
the country, and she was tempted to laugh and say, 'It's
me, Margaret, Owen. Doesn't that take you back a bit?'

More was to be extracted from Owen if she kept up the
pretence of being Charlotte. 'I don't suppose there's any
message from you I can give her.'

'Hm! Well! I've been thinking. I didn't tell you, Shah,
that when I was ill I saw her in a dream. Did I? No, well
why should I? It was more than a dream. It was a vision.
She was exactly as she was the time you were born. That
is to say, beautiful. And bright faced. The funny thing is
she was on an ocean liner. She said there was a Hunt Ball.
She was going to it and that is why she was in that lovely
dress and wearing those jewels in her ears.'

'Do you want me to tell her that?'

'No, it's all so silly. Just say I send her my love.'

'Love?'

'Yes, give her my love.'

'Would you like to see her?'

'Why not? Why not, Shah? Why not, my dear?'

'To ask why not doesn't make you sound all that eager.'

'You're right, my dear. I ought to be more positive. So
the question is why. What would the positive reason be
for a meeting? Let us think about it. She will have
changed. I have changed. I'm just a tired old man who
takes pills. No, from your mother's point of view there
would be no pleasure in the encounter.' She remembered
that Owen did not laugh much but, surprisingly, he was

laughing now, if that is what the high, tight, coughing sound signified. 'The conversation would be difficult. What would we talk about?'

'Cabbages and kings.'

'It would come to that. More to the point. Your mother would not want to see me, would she, Shah? Of course not. I understand that. But that makes no difference to the love I have for her.'

'I'd have thought you'd hate her.'

'No, Shah, we are all God's creatures lodged for a while here below. This is no permanent home. It is in the nature of things that, for me, time is short. Love is long. To misquote, we must love one another and die. Do you understand that, Shah? But you must do or you would not have decided on confirmation of your Christian beliefs.'

'I'm less sure of them.'

'What?'

'The way the world is. This bombing. But that's the least of the awful things that go on.'

'But Shah, I beg you. You said that what tipped the balance for you was a faith experience. I mean, you said you had this conviction come to you in a church with lighted candles. In spite of the awfulness you'd hang on to this experience. Giving and loving would be your answer. What you said made a deep impression on me. I'd never heard anyone talking quite like that of love as defiance. But it is. As Christ defied the Cross.'

'I guess being pregnant makes women say silly things.' Margaret did not even wonder whether she would get away with presenting Charlotte as a sceptic. Taunting Owen gave her so much malicious pleasure she did not stop to think what Owen and the real Charlotte would have to say to each other. 'As for Christ defying the

Cross,' she said, 'what he actually cried out was something about God forsaking him.'

'In the last agony, of course. But that was the beginning and not the end. Shah, you must listen to me. I've had a letter from your Michael Bellamy. He sounds a good man. You must speak to him openly. As you have spoken to me. Of course, I realise you are upset. After the experience you've had who wouldn't be? You must hold on to that experience you had. It was a sign of God's grace. You must believe me, my dear.'

Margaret wondered what Charlotte called her father. She could not risk calling him either father or Owen so decided to call him nothing at all. 'No, I don't really believe you. I have to say this. It's just being pregnant I talked like that. Otherwise I wouldn't have gone along with such nonsense.'

And she put the phone down.

5
Alexander

In spite of all the trouble he had caused, Alexander was the most beautiful baby born in the United Kingdom that year. Or anywhere, Daniel argued. Or, in Charlotte's opinion, ever. Even Tomas, who had seen quite a number of new-born babies, his half-brothers Stepan and Vilem for two, was less sure that Alexander was the universal and all-time prodigy that Daniel and Charlotte thought but he was ready to agree that his new half-brother was admirable; and, indeed, he did admire him, his jet eyes and pink little porcelain ears. The eyes were bold and enquiring not so much 'Who are *you*?' but 'Who do you think *I* am?' When Tibetan monks went in search of the latest incarnation of the Dalai Lama they looked in infants for evidence of precocious intelligence. They would certainly have found it in Alexander, Tomas thought.

Joy over Alexander made everyone forget Margaret's strange departure which had taken place some weeks before his arrival.

'She's annoyed about something,' said Charlotte. 'She's *that* displeased. Funny thing she won't out with it. She won't say what has gone wrong and that is not like Meg. She speaks her mind, usually.'

'She probably just wanted to get back home.' Daniel had not noticed anything amiss. 'She saw you were getting about again. Must have been boring for her just sitting around. So she took off. What's strange about that?'

After the bomb Charlotte spent ten days in the Clinic. The specialist had taken a good look and said there was no reason for her to be bedbound. The crisis was past. Whatever was supposed to hold was holding and she could take reasonable exercise. By this time Daniel had taken a short lease on a rather grand flat with three bedrooms, two bathrooms and a Scandinavian kitchen (that's what the agent called it) in Hanover Terrace with a view of the waters and greenery of Regent's Park. Pricey, but Wheatley-Minotaur picked up the tab. The Kensington flat had to be abandoned. Even if the bomb damage could have been put right quickly they did not like living there after what had happened; and the bomb damage was not going to be put right quickly. After Daniel had checked, so far as was possible, he would have no military or political VIPs as his new neighbours he decided to move straight in and Charlotte went direct from the Clinic. Margaret supervised the moving of their personal effects from Kensington and then announced she was making for Tampa.

'I feel I've been neglecting Simon,' she said.

She said how delighted she was that Charlotte was up and about again but otherwise had little to say for herself even when challenged.

'Wrong? There's nothing wrong. You're in good hands. This girl you've taken on seems very capable. It's a pity

152

now you're able to get about you don't come back to the States with me and have the baby there. But I can see Daniel's trapped here with this business racket – '

'It's not a racket.'

'Well, take-over or whatever. He's stuck here for the time being. So you are too. As for me, I just feel surplus to requirements.'

The girl Margaret referred to was a trained nannie from an agency called Betty Travers. The three of them, Margaret, Charlotte and the new nannie, made an outing together, the first for Charlotte since she had been laid up, buying the layette Charlotte had not been able to think about for fear something might go wrong. Len ferried them to and fro and would have been happy to go into John Lewis's and carry the parcels if only he had been able to park the car. There was a baby carriage to transport, too, and he could not have got that into the boot anyway. So the store would arrange for it to be delivered. Charlotte carried herself easily. Not much walking, certainly no climbing of stairs. She felt enormous but as there were lots of other equally ponderous women moving like tethered balloons round the baby departments this both-ered her not at all; to every eye she was obviously two people. Only she was aware there was a third.

The day Margaret was to fly back to the States Charlotte went with her. Len drove them to Heathrow, parked the car and prepared to carry the luggage over to the terminal while Charlotte said goodbye to her mother. 'It's been wonderful having you here, Meg.' And so on.

But Margaret was not so effusive in return and Char-lotte once more felt she or Daniel must unwittingly have offended her but try as she did could get no clue what it might be. In fact Margaret snubbed her. 'You'll be O.K. Everything will be O.K. I know that. Now I just want you to concentrate on having this baby and forget about me. Don't think about me at all. I'll call you to say I've arrived safe and sound. Naturally I'll be eager for your news. But let's wait for it, shall we? Call me when the baby's born. But not until.' A quick kiss. No hug.

And she was off, Len wheeling her three great suitcases, two holdalls and a hatbox on a trolley, walking through the drizzly morning without looking back. Charlotte gazed after her with tears running down her face. She was glad Meg was going. Her bad mood had been upsetting and Charlotte could not cope with it in her state of pregnancy. Back in Florida Meg would cheer up and they would have the same comfortable long telephone conversations they had in the past; and who knew? she'd be back to see Alexander. Charlotte hoped so, anyway, but it did not stop her from crying.

'I ribbed her about her boy friend,' said Daniel. 'But she seemed to take it in her stride.'

'You did what?'

'This guy she met on the plane. What was his name? Edgar something.'

'What about him?'

'He was going on this cruise and she was all for going too. I notice these things, Char. I've got antennae. Yeah, she was just wild to go. Then nothing happened.'

'What do you mean, you ribbed her about her boy friend?'

'It was all good fun. I'm all in favour of old women having a fling. Tones them up. So I said something about, you know, romance in the air.'

'You shouldn't have done that, Daniel. That's just awful.'

'What's awful about telling a woman she's made a conquest?'

'But it's all rubbish. Meg isn't like that. She's about to be a grandmother, for God's sake! When did all this happen? When I was in the Clinic? No wonder she took offence. Oh, why did you have to do this? I could scream! I really could! Did you take a look at that man Edgar? Meg would be the last person to fall for a man with a long nose like that. And that silly grin. I guess it was you thinking a guy like that could stir her up, that is what upset her. So that's what she's been so uptight about! You know what I think? You've really boobed. And how!'

She was so angry she wanted to do something to demonstrate her feelings. She was sitting and he was standing so she could not hit him and there was no glass or porcelain object to hand she could hurl to the ground and smash. It was particularly infuriating that he could not understand her fury, or even see that she really was furious, any more than he would have understood how offensive he had been to Meg. She would have liked to call Meg and apologise. But that was impossible. She would not even have arrived at Tampa yet. But even if Charlotte called tomorrow or the next day just how would she go about apologising? The apology would have to come from Daniel and he simply did not understand there was anything to be apologetic about.

'I wouldn't have mentioned this,' he said, 'but you kept on about not knowing why Meg was so awful and I felt I had to come up with something to set your mind at rest. It's not good enough because Meg didn't react the way you're imagining. But it may have needled her more than I thought. I grant you that. Now look, kid. I'm sorry to have upset you but I honestly don't think I've been such a bum as you say. Course, it's true I forgot to pass on that message.'

'What message?'

'This guy Edgar called one evening when Meg wasn't here. He wanted to speak to her so I took the message which was that he was back from his trip but he'd be leaving for the States the next day. It slipped my mind. Well, I've got preoccupations. There are problems in the office. They're problems that run around in the mind like mice. But it isn't as though I told Meg when it was too late. I didn't tell her at all. It's only when we started talking I remember this man calling so she can't even know I didn't pass his message on. She can't be holding that against us. Maybe she doesn't hold anything against us and that what she's got is a bad belly ache, or something.'

'I take that personally.'

'She was expecting that call from Edgar.'

'Hi! So I wasn't that much off beam!'

'Meg would not have done anything wrong.'

Daniel went and looked out of the window at the park which seemed theatrical in the evening sunshine. Almost operatic. It was the way the light caught the lightly coloured roses, the whites and the yellows. People drifted this way and that. Lots of children. Oh, and all those ducks on the water were scurrying about, chasing bits of bread no doubt. Cue for an orchestra, entry of the chorus and a lead singer, tenor dressed as what? a soldier in a red uniform with gold epaulettes. That was the sort of thing that really interested him. In comparison this talk about Meg was boring. Wasn't it time for him to show spirit?

'It's my belief, Char, she'd have been away on this cruise with the long-nosed and grinning Edgar if it hadn't been for the bomb.'

'What's that got to do with it?'

'It stopped her in her tracks. She's mean but she's not

so mean she could turn her back on us after we'd had our place blown up.'

'That's a disgraceful thing to say about my mother.'

'Funny thing is I don't believe Meg would consider it disgraceful.'

It was the first real row they had had since – well, it must have been when he had tickets for *Don Carlos* and she decided at the last minute she was not going. Take your secretary, she had said, or somebody, and he had claimed to be more annoyed by that suggestion than her flunking out of the opera. The box office gave him cash for the returned ticket. It must have been bought by the little woman wearing perfume so powerful it made his eyes smart who sat next to him; a story, as a way of keeping the row going, she affected not to believe. She had rather enjoyed it. Her point about opera had been conclusively made.

Daniel tried to calm her but she would not be calmed. Her anger was like a fire in parched undergrowth that moved fast and pounced on anything combustible. Daniel's various failings came up for review and the one she fastened on, quite unfairly, was his treatment of Tomas. It had nothing to do with Daniel's clumsiness over Meg; but that only went to show how she could find a weak spot when she wanted to.

'And another thing – ' she shouted.

'Char! Please!'

'Have you spoken to Tomas recently? Don't you care? His trainee job at the theatre isn't being funded any more. So he's out of work but for the radio work and that doesn't pay enough to live on.'

'O.K. you know I'd bail him out but he won't have it.'

'He doesn't want just bailing out. He's a clever kid. He ought to go to college.'

'Would he go?'

'Sure he'd go. He's got a girl friend too. I don't suppose you even knew that. She told him the way he keeps talking about books he ought to go to college. And he buys that. He really buys that, Daniel.'

Talking about Tomas did what Daniel could not. It calmed her. He was so glad of the respite he would have been ready to talk about Tomas for the rest of the evening; what it came into his head to say, however, Charlotte met with silence. She had to stop and think.

'That's something your father might help with. He might pull strings at his college.'

The row had stirred Charlotte up so much that all sorts of odd fragments came to the surface of her mind; the half-forgotten face appeared of a kid she had once dated, a certain Rudi who wore dark glasses and wanted to join the navy which she thought he probably did. Then there was the occasion, soon after they married, Daniel and she called in on Meg and Simon – they were on their way back from their Caribbean honeymoon – and Meg said how wonderful it was to see her so happy but she ought to remember first marriages often did not work out.

'Don't put all your chips on that one number. The wheel spins and other numbers come up.'

It was the first indication of hostility to Daniel but there were others as time went by. Charlotte even fancied she might be working to undermine her marriage, then put the thought aside as just too silly. What possible reason would there be? Meg's niggling criticism of Daniel stopped as soon as Charlotte became pregnant but she thought of it now and did not wonder that Daniel had stirred up more than he could imagine.

She told herself to be calm. No, it was not quite that. She was not telling herself anything; Alexander was there inside her and there was this extra presence too. This extra presence was telling her what to do and so insistently it was a command. Be patient. There is no need to concern yourself. All will be well. All things will be well. She was so relaxed she could tell Daniel thought she had forgiven him and the row was really over. She hadn't really forgiven him but stayed quiet, just as the extra presence ordered, she smiled, she kissed him back warmly and was genuinely happy with the flowers – of penitence he called them – that he went out and bought, next day, peach coloured roses with lots of maidenhair fern. Charlotte was pleased to trim the stems and place the roses in the silver bowl that came with the flat and signed for on the inventory.

And Tomas? The mood Meg was in it was surprising she had not made more use of Tomas as evidence against Daniel. Charlotte had already warned her off the subject and if she came back to it a line would be firmly drawn. Daniel had behaved honourably and was ready to act generously. All credit to him. Her inner voice was beginning to tell her Daniel should be given the opportunity to earn even more credit by financing the boy through college.

'I'll write to my father,' she said. 'I need to give him our new address anyway. I don't suppose he even knew about our bomb.'

When Meg telephoned to report she was safely back in Tampa she surprised Charlotte by asking whether she had heard from her father; this in a neutral sort of voice as though she was asking about some casual acquaintance and not the near-malign figure she conjured up on the rare occasions she could bring herself to mention him.

'Since you mention it, no,' said Charlotte and Meg went straight on to talk about Simon's plan to take her off on some trip in connection with his Sci-Fi research, as

though mentioning Owen was of no consequence whatsoever. Normally she would not have allowed a mention
of him without some hostile remark but not this time.
Nothing! Charlotte was intrigued by this and was half-
tempted to ring Oxford straight away and thought better
of it when she remembered her father's dislike of
telephones.

So she wrote, giving the new address and telling him
about the bomb. Just in case he was still disappointed she
and Daniel were not going to have their marriage blessed
in the college chapel she said certain thoughts had come to
her about the church and she was being prepared for
confirmation by the Rev. Michael Bellamy who was
continuing to visit her in their new home and was such an
admirer of the articles he wrote in the *Courier*. She
described the view they had of the park. No mention of
Meg. She told him about the gynaecological checks and
said everything now pointed to the successful arrival of
his grandson but hoped he would remember him in his
prayers. There were signs that Daniel's spell in London
would wind up before the end of the year. They certainly
hoped to spend Christmas, all three of them, back in New
York but before that she promised to bring Alexander to
Oxford for inspection and approval. Before ending with
enquiries about his own health and saying she hoped he
was getting enough exercise she brought up the subject of
a brilliant young Czech student she and Daniel knew. He
was a political refugee with no real career prospects unless
he could get a college place. He had mentioned the London
School of Economics. But what were prospects like at
Oxford these days? Tomas really was brilliant. He was
quite outstanding at chess. She had played with him and
it was uncanny the way he did not seem to have to think
about his moves but they were always ones she would

never have thought of. Yet when he made them they were so obviously right. He was quite a genius. Charlotte sent her greeting to Aunt Eleanor.

Owen had just returned from posting his *Courier* article which he was so pleased with he pulled out the carbon copy and read it through again. He had called it 'In Praise of Women'. When the rest of his disciples deserted Jesus at his arrest, and Peter denied that he even knew him, the women remained faithful. They, and not the men, watched the crucifixion and after the resurrection found the tomb empty. So said Mark, the earliest and most straightforward account of what happened. Men should reverence women not only for what they were and the natural spirituality so many were capable of but also because of the Biblical evidence. One thing was sure. Men and women were different and the difference was to be cherished. No one, Owen reflected, could call him (what was the horrid expression?) a male chauvinist pig.

Charlotte's letter arrived by the second post and he read it with bewilderment. He had been saddened by her rejection over the telephone of whatever religious belief she was struggling towards and then cheered by the thought she must have been upset by the bomb and was speaking wildly. Only his worry over the bomb had prompted him to telephone, so much did he dislike using it, and there was no question of a second call. He was put off writing by the fear of another snub. A letter to Michael Bellamy might appear to be going behind her back. Margaret was with her, she said. Perhaps she had been a bad influence. And then this letter came, written as though there had been no talk between them.

He read it again. Perhaps his mind was not working as

well as it should. Certainly he was more forgetful. Of that he was well aware but this bewilderment over Charlotte might be a sign of something more serious. Brain cells could deteriorate. The *Courier* would drop him. Eleanor would come to make sure he dressed properly. Women lived longer than men, Eleanor seemed eternal and the time might be at hand when, God forbid, she would take him in hand, insist he moved into what he believed was called sheltered accommodation where there was a warden and bells to press when help was needed. A worse possibility would be if Eleanor herself decided to be the warden and lodge him in her own cottage where her friends Molly Prince and Betty Folkes could come and jolly him along.

Charlotte's unexpected re-entry into his life had been a joy. What she said on the telephone was all the more upsetting because of the hopes she had raised. In his gloom he began to consider, for the first time, whether the fault lay in himself; why else could he be so unlucky with women? First of all Eleanor, the domineering sister, then Margaret the unfaithful wife and now Charlotte, the capricious daughter. He even thought of the girl in the Mickey Mouse jumper who stole his wallet. Why in spite of all the evidence against women did he remain the man who wrote such articles as the one that lay on the floor in front of him where the sheets had fallen from his hand?

When he made his mind blank in preparation for prayer the word Woman had a way of appearing, as though in a screen only to dissolve and the image of someone, certainly not Margaret, appear. The image was clouded. He would not have been able to recognise it but for knowing that it was his mother, smiling and kissing him, thanking him for the pretty French picture he had not been able to give her in life but now in the world of dreams could lovingly hand over. Or was it just a green-lined parasol? That was the woman he wrote in praise of.

My dear Shah,

I had no news of you for so long but your letter, which has just arrived, was not unexpected. Although ashamed of the fact I am superstitious about birds. There has, of late, been a surprising increase in the magpie population and I often see some of them prancing about in the garden strip opposite. Yesterday four magpies were there. This is a sign of a birth. Did you know that? In the spring when the blue tits are so active they actually come and peck at my window panes as though they are trying to break in. And now, out of season, one has been tapping at my window for days on and off. This could mean only one thing – a letter. And that is why yours was not unexpected.

I rejoice that you are comfortable in a new home after your terrible bomb experience. Thank God it was no worse. And thank God too that what the four magpies foretold is developing auspiciously though I do not understand why you are sure it will be a boy. You are certainly in my prayers and I feel all the better for uttering them on behalf of you, your child and your husband.

My health is reasonable and I could easily come to London and spare you the journey here. All you have to do is give the signal. The train service is excellent and I could get a cab at Paddington. That you are, in your situation, still being prepared for confirmation is heart-warming and I pray for you on that account too.

Your young Czech friend sounds interesting. I am

out of touch with the admissions procedure here nowadays but why not suggest that he write to the Master of St Ebbe's College, giving information about the studies he has made in his homeland and what he might wish to read in Oxford? I suggest the Master because he is a Czech too. Dr Sir Karl Strauss would be interested in a political refugee from Czechoslovakia because he was one himself many years ago. When next I see him I shall mention that you have, as it seems, rather taken this boy under your wing. Entry to a college is much competed for nowadays. That has to be borne in mind.

I will certainly give your greetings to your Aunt Eleanor. I had not thought of her as an aunt before and it puts her in a new light. You did not mention your mother. If she is still with you remember me kindly to her.

Your affectionate father
Owen Bark

Charlotte showed this letter to Tomas, saying it was delightful and asking him to admire the neat calligraphic hand it was written in; real ink, obviously, and very black. The lettering was small but beautifully executed so it could be read as easily as print. Not only was it a pleasure to look at, the contents pleased her too, though the reference to Meg puzzled her a little. No matter. She came to regard the letter as an important step along the path Tomas would take, though he himself did not see it in quite that way. Of more importance was the bomb and the questions this caused him to ask about the Irish Republican Army.

Charlotte and Daniel seemed to accept the bomb as some natural misfortune like being struck by lightning;

they did not even say how terrible it was and what awful people the terrorists must be. Tomas was more curious. Back in Prague everyone had heard of the IRA and it was assumed they were patriotic Irishmen trying to drive the occupying British troops out of Ireland, rather as Czechs would like to drive the Russians out of Czechoslovakia. In the Bush House canteen Josh Smilan said it was not like that at all and Tomas said, 'Well, what is it like then? The Arabs in Palestine?' No, said Josh, that was quite different. So were the Basques in Spain. In Northern Ireland there were savage tribal differences and unless British troops were there to try and keep the peace there would be wholesale murder. Tomas was not convinced by this and tried to develop a theory about the inevitability of terrorism whenever a dominant power, like Germany had been, the Soviet Union now was in Eastern Europe, had weaker neighbours. These weaker neighbours were a threat to security because they could provide footholds for hostile powers. England and Ireland were a bit like that. First the Spanish, then the French had tried to invade through Ireland, so naturally the English took counter-measures, some of them very brutal. Power was what counted. Take *King Lear*. Shakespeare had made a mistake in pinning the story on such human failings as pride and ambition. The real issue was the political instability Lear created by his bogus abdication and the way everybody else scurried to find positions of strength. The threat of instability was what caused wars and terrorism.

'You're crazy,' said Josh. '*Lear* isn't that sort of play at all. It's about a man being destroyed by his own bad qualities.'

'That's what I'm saying. Shakespeare wrote the wrong play. It's too black. At the end it's about even love being useless. That's Shakespeare's story but the politics of it are more serious than that.'

'You're confused, Tomas. And ill-informed. Pick up some education and get yourself sorted out.'

That is why Tomas thought the bomb steered him into college and not anything Charlotte said, or any response she won from his father, not even the accident that Dr Karl Strauss happened to be a Czech too. Zoë may even have had more to do with it than Charlotte. She was Fred Bean's secretary at the Old Yard, had long piano-playing fingers and a languorous manner. She was not all that older than Tomas and giggled a great deal when he was near her. She was taking a degree in sociology at Birkbeck and told him it was a blessing his funding was ending because he was not cut out for show business; he ought to be taking a longer view. What would he be doing in a year's time? Two years' time? Three?

Josh had contacts at LSE. He made soundings and came back with the answer there was no hope of a place in the coming term. Bill Franks, who was head of the Czech section, knew Karl Strauss and established that the same answer would come from St Ebbe's. No matter how suitable he was, and that had to be established, his only course was to find himself a crammer and hope to win a place in the next academic year.

A more immediate preoccupation was the birth of Alexander which the child put off for as long as he could manage. This, after the initial anxiety that he might be a miscarriage, seemed to indicate indecisiveness and could be a pointer to his future character. First one thing and then the opposite, that is the kind of decision-maker he would prove and Daniel did not think this vacillation came from his side of the family. When Charlotte went to the Clinic under the misapprehension she was in labour

Danielaccompanied her and slept on a stretcher in the corridor because he had decided to be present at the birth. The stretcher was so uncomfortable that when Charlotte was sent home he insisted on a cubicle for the return visit and this is where, in fact, he was fast asleep when Alexander was delivered at two in the morning because the midwife forgot to wake him. Or, more likely, because Charlotte had given instructions that he was not to be wakened. She recognised that his wish to be present was an expression of wanting to be as intimately involved as a father could be. She appreciated his concern but thought Alexander's birth was too intimate a matter for that kind of sharing. As it was an experience she had not been through before she had no confidence of putting up the show that would win Daniel's approval, she might have no dignity whatsoever. The first sight Daniel had of his son was a pink, fish-like creature on the other side of a glass panel, dabbed over with talcum powder.

Owen had made it clear he wanted no delay over seeing his grandson. When the time came Daniel would not hear of his making the journey by train and sent Len down to pick him up in the company car. He brought great-aunt Eleanor as well, which no one had expected, so there was quite a gathering for lunch in Hanover Terrace. Daniel had found a *cordon bleu* chef who came in and prepared the meal in the Scandinavian kitchen; vichyssoise, smoked salmon, lamb cutlets, lemon soufflé, and, for simplicity, champagne throughout the meal. Nothing elaborate. Mrs Drewitt, the temporary housekeeper, served, though with some difficulty because great-aunt Eleanor decided she wanted to help too. She kept her hat on throughout, a green straw with a three inch brim and a feather in the band, which gave the impression that the slightest resistance to her ministrations would cause her to leave in a huff.

Tomas, wearing a Breton jumper and jeans, was there too. A place for Betty, the nanny, was found at the end of the table on the understanding that on the least sound from the nursery she would drop her knife and fork and rush out. The silver rose bowl, flamboyant with the most assertively-coloured blooms Daniel could find, cinnabar red, was in the middle of the table. Charlotte, at the head in grey slacks and a white jumper which were, *absolutely*, the only clothes she had that fitted, raised her glass in response to the toast Daniel was proposing, 'To Alexander, God bless him,' and added that she hoped to see them all again at the christening.

Owen had enjoyed his drive from Oxford. It was his first trip to London since before he went into hospital. The countryside had a late summer glow upon it, the hedgerows almost voluptuously green and the trees displaying themselves in the sun like banners. Didcot power station sent out whole Himalayas of white vapour. Eleanor was mercifully silent, busy with the *Times* crossword. He was really excited at the thought of seeing Alexander and not at all daunted by the possibility, no likelihood, that Margaret would be there too. Long ago he had given up his clerical collar and now wore a silvery tie with a blue stripe which had won even Eleanor's approval; a pleasant contrast to his dark suit. The new tablets seemed to be working. The doctor had said they were ACE inhibitors, whatever that meant, and they would have a longer term beneficial effect than the tablets he had been taking. Certainly he felt brighter, particularly in the mornings. All the better to enjoy this wonderful lunch. Except for the lemon soufflé and the rather splendid sauce that went with the cutlets, there was nothing a diabetic could refuse. Thank God he had such a good appetite for the smoked salmon and such pleasure in drinking his glass of Veuve Clicquot. Who was the young man in the Breton jumper? They had been introduced but Owen had forgotten already.

And still Owen had not seen his grandson. The child was sleeping and Charlotte did not want the risk of waking him. When the expected whimper came Betty was on her feet and away, followed impetuously by Owen who pushed his chair back so violently it fell over and Charlotte had to shout at him, 'Not yet, father. He'll need changing.'

Everyone laughed at Owen's embarrassment. This was increased when Owen saw that Daniel had his video recorder trained on him, ensuring that his discomfiture would be seen well in the future, by Alexander himself no doubt when he was old enough.

'I want to get a shot of you, sir, seeing Alexander for the first time. So I'll go right in there. Betty will give a shout when it's O.K. for you to make your entrance. It's like a movie. I feel like a real director, you know that, Charlotte?'

Not only did Daniel capture the moment when Owen, Eleanor close behind, looked down with wonder and joy at his grandson – face like a little budding rose, he thought – but the even more stirring moment when Charlotte appeared, picked Alexander up, and placed him in her father's arms. The child so light, a mere flake of humanity, who looked up in puzzlement and then – yes, surely it was a smile! Owen stood as erect and as still as he could manage. Not only was he moved more than it had been possible to imagine but his body felt at its back the gentle probing he had first experienced in the Botanic Garden hot house just before that girl in the Mickey Mouse jumper had appeared. How terrible if he had an attack just at that moment! Then the probing stopped, thanks no doubt to these new ACE inhibitors he was taking, he was freed from pain and tension and out of simple gratitude for that and for the sight of the treasure he was holding in his arms tears came. He was quite unashamed. Daniel still had the video camera trained on him but Owen did not mind. He had thought tears of joy was just an expression because he had never seen any, certainly never felt any coursing down his own worn cheeks, so they could be real too! *Nunc Dimittis*. If that was not an impiety.

Charlotte pulled up her white jumper to feed Alexander. 'Don't go away,' she said.

She sat on a low chair. Betty transferred the baby from Owen to her lap. She released her full breast and the baby, making little snorting noises, fastened on to her and Charlotte looked down with a grave smile on her face.

'He's so greedy.' As though in astonishment Alexander stopped sucking and appeared to look up at her. 'There, there. I meant it kindly. I'm *pleased* you're greedy, sweetheart.'

Back in the dining room the chef had appeared with cream and a pot of coffee. He tried to tempt Owen to a brandy but Owen said no, just a black coffee without sugar which he drank standing at the window looking out over the park. It was mellow, sunny September out there and he could not look at the flowered bushes and the trees stirring, catching the light in the light breeze, without a sob rising and threatening to break. This moment might be his fulfilment. What else had his life led to but this moment? He could ask for no greater happiness.

'You look tired,' said Eleanor. 'Are you sure you're all right?'

'Never felt better.' Adding, 'In a manner of speaking.'

He was glad, nevertheless, to be led into the little sitting room where he could sink into a comfortable chair and be offered some more coffee by that young man in the Breton jumper who said Charlotte could not have been kinder to him if she had been his own mother.

'She wrote to you about me going to college.'

So this was the young Czech Charlotte had befriended and, really, he ought to have guessed as much because of his foreign accent. What was his name? Tomas. Tomas what? Tomas Rais. Yes, it so happened that Owen had seen Karl Strauss and mentioned the case of Charlotte's protegé. How had Tomas come to England and was he not unhappy at being separated from his family?

'Do you mind if I smoke?' Without waiting for an answer Daniel lit a small cigar and sat on the arm of Tomas's chair. In his black and white tiny-checked slacks and short-sleeved shirt he looked as though he had just come in from the beach. The shirt had a pattern of brightly coloured tropical fruits and flowers so it might have been no ordinary beach, it was a beach of the whitest coral sand. He was flushed with the excitement of the occasion, possibly from the champagne too. When he spoke ocean breakers seemed to whisper in the background. He patted Tomas on the shoulder.

'Tomas is my son, sir. Alexander's half-brother.'

Owen was slow to take this in. 'I didn't know you have been married before.'

'No, that's not how it was. Charlotte's the only girl I've been married to and that's the way it's going to stay. Yes, I believe in the institution of marriage. Didn't Charlotte tell you about Tomas? He's a bastard and I'm not ashamed of it.'

Daniel liked an audience when he was talking. Having settled Alexander down, Betty was there, so was Mrs

171

Drewitt and even the chef in his white hat and apron who at Daniel's insistence was relaxing with them after the meal with a glass of champagne. Charlotte was lying on the settee with her eyes closed and Eleanor sat with a little table in front of her bearing a tray of chocolate mints which she steadily ate through.

The flat was not furnished in the way the Blairs would have chosen but it had to be put up with. Certainly it was all very English – the William Morris covers, the needle-work screen in front of the bogus fireplace and the button upholstery of the settee where Charlotte reclined; the afternoon light from the tall windows was English too in the way it alternately blossomed and faded as the clouds passed over the sun. Daniel's exotic behaviour seemed all the odder because of the setting; he was being not at all English, quite outlandish from Eleanor's point of view. But then he was American and unpredictable. It put one in mind of one of those Italian gatherings one saw on holidays where everyone in a public place, friends, acquaintances, passers-by, even the waiters, joined in some family row. Daniel waved his cigar and blew out smoke from his moist, full lips while everyone, in varying states of interest and surprise, listened to his views. Young men had fun. Young women too. All had been for the best.

'Don't you agree, Tomas?'

Tomas was so angry at this public exposure that he did not know what to say and Charlotte called over languidly, 'Oh, do stop it, Daniel, for heaven's sake!'

'I just wanted everybody to know where we all stood.'

Tomas rose abruptly from his chair and accidentally knocked Daniel's cigar out of his hand. Dnaiel scrambled after it before it could burn the carpet. The chef, Mrs Drewitt and Betty seemed to take this as a signal for withdrawal, realising the talk had not been meant for them. Daniel did not care. Their presence had given extra resonance to what he said; and now he was laughing and stuffing the cigar back into his mouth.

'Say, this is turning out to be quite a party. Sir,' he said to Owen, 'there's nothing in your glass. I can't stand seeing undrunk champagne.'

Tomas walked out of the room but Charlotte was up from her settee and after him. Their raised voices could be heard coming back from the dining room where she had caught up with him and seized him by the arm.

'No, you really can't go like that.'

'But he's so *disgusting*.'

'No, no, no. *Please*, Tomas.' She appeared in the doorway. 'You've got to apologise to him, Daniel.'

'What for? I thought the kid would be pleased.'

Charlotte had turned and was shouting, 'Tomas, Tomas,' so the boy was clearly still on his way and Owen found himself strangely excited.

'Owen! Where are you going?' Eleanor was not going to allow any excitement if she could possibly stop it but Owen was already on his feet and moving towards the dining room with such speed and lightness of bearing he might have been borne by invisible hands. In spite of the rumpus Daniel had created Owen was still aloft on the emotional upsurge that seeing and holding Alexander had released. In his euphoria he was capable of achieving just about anything. Wonders were there for the starting up. In spite of his afflictions and the years of groping, so inadequately, for something he could lay his hands on and know to be rock-bottom truth, he had been spared for this hour and that was a wonder in itself.

'Tomas,' he called. The strangeness of his rather cracked voice rather than any note of authority made Tomas turn at the door leading to the hall and Owen was able to catch up with him.

'If you go, Tomas,' he said, 'it will break Charlotte's heart.'

Had he gone too far? Charlotte was at the other end of the dining room and she might not have agreed to that way of putting it. Owen sensed, though, that whatever he said had to be dramatic. Otherwise Tomas would not only go but the breach with his father would be irreparable. All this had been revealed to Owen as though by angels. This boy, whom he had not seen until a couple of hours ago; and not known, until a few minutes ago was – what? Charlotte's step-son and, in a sense, his own step-grandson? – had to be held.

'At least, I think it will,' he now added.

Tomas hesitated. 'I can't be all that important.'

In the silence they could hear a window rattling in the wind and traffic noises. Not only was it quiet in the flat but everyone stood still, Tomas with a slightly scared, hunted expression on his face, Owen with one hand on his shoulder, Charlotte and Eleanor at the other end of the room standing side by side and Daniel in the doorway looking like one of those smiling, unflappable baddies in the movies who could be relied on to make his escape in the end and leave the way open for a money-spinning sequel.

They could also hear Alexander crying.

Tomas rushed to Charlotte in such distress she took him in her arms. 'I can't bear it,' he said.

'It's all right, Tomas. Nothing has changed.'

'Forgive me.'

'*That's my boy*,' said Daniel with a chuckle.

★

Len had been driving them for some time on the journey back to Oxford and not making a lot of progress because of the traffic when Eleanor, while still looking straight ahead, said 'Well, I must say you made a bit of a fool of yourself, Owen.'

'I don't look at it like that.'

The excitement had drained him and he did not want an argument with Eleanor. He could not let her remark pass, though. He had not been a fool. He had behaved well and Charlotte herself had told him so.

'Why you felt called on to interfere is past my comprehension, Owen. Who are you to back up behind Charlotte's husband, what's his name?, and that boy? It might have been a good thing for him to walk out. Who are you to say? Who is Charlotte to say, for that matter? What's his name? Daniel. If you ask me he wanted to see the back of that boy and that is what he was playing for all the time. Otherwise his behaviour would be quite inexplicable. That's what all his ranting was in aid of. I don't see how he could have an illegitimate Czech son, anyway.'

Eleanor was a great reader of spy stories and now her enthusiasm took over. 'Perhaps he was seduced by a beautiful special agent. Such things happen. Behind the Iron Curtain temptations are often put in the way of visiting business men.'

In spite of his weariness Owen was strengthened by the knowledge that Charlotte had thanked him for what he had done. Mrs Drewitt had been clearing up in the dining room, the chef was packing up in the kitchen, Betty was in the nursery and Daniel was talking to Tomas in the sitting room, giving him jokey punches in the stomach to show he had no hard feelings, so the only place Charlotte could have a word with her father in private was the bedroom which, did Owen but know it, had been Margaret's.

'You were wonderful,' Charlotte told him. 'Tomas is sensitive and the thought of him going off like that was just too awful. I could never have stopped him by myself. Everyone was just amazed by what you did. It was so unexpected, and so wonderful. I had no idea you were like that.' And she kissed him on the cheek.

'He's fond of you. That's not remarkable. You're somebody it's easy to be fond of. His fondness is like that of a son for his mother. Always cherish him, my dear.'

She was startled by his vehemence. 'Sure I'll cherish him so far as he lets me. Daniel's son has to be my son.'

'It's more than cherish. He will need you. A man needs a mother, God knows.' The French painting of the seaside with the woman holding a green parasol floated before his eyes. 'Happiness is like dew. It goes up in the morning sun. But while it is there, rejoice.'

Plainly, he was very moved and she could not understand why. He might have been responding to a voice he could hear but nobody else could. 'You took us all by surprise.'

'Something drove me. Happiness, I think. It was most mysterious.'

'So it was Alexander's doing really.'

'Yes, and the happiness of knowing that what you said on the telephone was all behind you.'

Charlotte was puzzled anew. He could see this and had to remind her. There she had been, in that bombed flat, talking not at all like her real self because she was still in a state of such shock. 'That was the way of it, wasn't it?'

'But I didn't talk to you on the telephone. I was out of the flat before the bomb went off and I never went back.'

But Meg had.

176

She remembered the reference to Meg in his magpie letter and how this had puzzled her because, so far as she knew, he had been unaware that Meg was in the country. Certainly she had not told him. Meg had made it clear she disapproved of Charlotte seeing her father and this disapproval would probably extend to giving any information that might lead to annoyance; Owen writing to her or even trying to get in touch. Nevertheless Owen had known she was there. How?

Thinking about all this she repeated herself in a dazed sort of way. 'That's right. I went to the casualty reception at some hospital and then Daniel insisted I went straight off to the Clinic. I never went back to the flat.'

'I certainly spoke to someone and she sounded like you. The voice did. Not what was said.'

'It must have been my mother. Because she went back.'

'So.' Owen had deliberated. 'It is very strange that after all these years I should speak to your mother and that she should choose to pretend she was you. If indeed that is what happened.'

'What did she say?'

Owen had shrugged because he was confused. If Charlotte was right he had learned something that was both welcome and unwelcome at the same time. He preferred not to think of the wounding bit in order to dwell on what was good. 'She said – that is to say, I thought *you* said, you were less sure of your Christian beliefs. I think she said they were nonsense.'

'She said that?'

'But now I know that was simply Margaret talking. Oh, the difference!'

'She must have known all this would come out. How silly of her! And how – *wicked*!' Charlotte had stared at him, her mouth set hard. Her face had coloured and Owen had wanted to put out a hand and touch her, to comfort her because of the realisation that she had been hurt even more than he had.

He did not know that Charlotte was all the more angry because of the realisation this deception of Meg's lay behind the dark mood of her last days with them. It was guilt and, by God, she was right to feel guilty!

'You must never tell your mother we've had this conversation.'

Charlotte had looked at him in bewilderment. Then she relaxed and even smiled. 'I'm not sure that's the really charitable thing to do, but I know what you mean. I've got to be Christian about it. That's hard. But even if you'd not said it my voice would. Now Alexander is born I'm back to being alone with it.'

On that drive with Eleanor back to Oxford Owen fell asleep and dreamed he was in some strange town with that young Czech. They went from house to house searching for someone but it was hopeless. Owen asked who they were looking for and the young Czech said it was his mother. No sign of her. Either the houses were empty or the people in them had never heard of this woman they were looking for. Owen became very anxious about their failure and when Eleanor woke him he was glad to escape from the dream. She said the driver wanted to know if he could put the radio on so that he could listen to the football results.

'Of course,' said Owen, rousing himself at last. For some time they listened to the results and Len made his comments.

'Do you follow any team?' Owen asked. 'Newcastle perhaps.'

'Ah! You can tell by my Geordie accent. Best in the country or they would be if it wasn't for the board. They

178

sell all the good players. Bobby Charlton would've played for Newcastle but the board was too daft to see it. He went off to Man United. What's your team, then?'

'Arsenal.'

'Boring Arsenal. They get results but they're boring. There y'are! Hear that? Drew with Everton nil-nil. Typical Arsenal result that. Sorry to say it, but they're boring.'

'If you pick on a team you stay with them.'

'That's true, sir.'

Len was taking them through the new cutting on the edge of the Chilterns. Once they were past the white walls they could see the sere autumnal plain opening up before them.

The evening before Owen's operation a house-surgeon came up to the ward and explained what would happen. A very fine tube with an inflatable nozzle, a kind of catheter, would be inserted in an artery, probably at a point in the groin. It would be eased up the artery until the end was, under X-ray control, right up against the clot at that point in the heart that was causing the angina. It was called an atheroma and the cause of the pain Owen was experiencing. The surgeon would use a syringe to inflate the nozzle like a little balloon, to bring pressure on the atheroma and stretch the coronary artery which had narrowed. The aim was to disperse that clot and so relieve the cardiac system. O.K.? Nothing to it.

'Sounds terrifying,' said Owen.

'But it isn't really.'

'Has it been done before, I mean, I'm not a guinea pig?'

'We do several a week. You don't even need an anaesthetic.'

Owen was not worried by the prospect but he needed

an assurance the surgeon knew what he was doing. 'As a procedure it sounds a bit unlikely. Surely there is some-thing a bit more sophisticated. It sounds like the sweeper's brush up a chimney.'

The house-surgeon said that was the way it was and he could expect to be taken down to the theatre at 8 a.m. The surgeon would be Mr Ibrahim Badawi. Get some sleep. On second thoughts perhaps a sleeping tablet would be in order.

Owen said no thank you, he never had difficulty in sleeping and had settled down to gaze at the ceiling and concentrate his thoughts on something agreeable, the Arsenal team running out on to a sunny field, to start with, and looking frisky in their claret shirts and white shorts, when he was amazed to find Charlotte at his bedside, looking down at him and smiling.

'Good heavens. How did you get here?'

'Train. How are you feeling?'

'I'm fine really. But why have you come?' She undid her coat and sat down, seemingly reassured to find him not looking so sick as she expected. 'Have you brought the baby with you?'

'Betty is looking after Alexander. It will be part of the weaning. Just as well. I'm not the milch cow I ought to be.' But she gave off a milky, vanilla kind of perfume as though to deny what she said and Owen marvelled that this female and fecund creature was his daughter, flesh of his flesh. 'Aunt Eleanor called me this afternoon. That's why I'm here. They're very relaxed about visiting hours, I must say.'

'Very nice for me, Shah. But you must have put yourself out and there is no need. What will Daniel think?'

'As soon as he knew you were having open-heart surgery, he said he'd be glad for me to come.'

'But there's no question of open-heart surgery. Is that what your aunt said? That was silly of her. It's just a cardiac angioplasty.'

'What's that?'

Rather proud of having remembered the name of the operation mentioned by the house-surgeon, Owen tried to describe it as well as he could. Charlotte realised it was nothing like so drastic as open heart surgery and said, 'Oh, I'm so glad. Why did Aunt Eleanor get it wrong?'

'Ignorance, I expect. She's always so fit I suspect she thinks the human body is just solid inside and the very idea of exploring it would be confusing for her.'

'She said you had angina.'

'There's a clot they're going to get rid of. But Shah, I'm very touched you should come and see me even if it is on false pretences.'

Charlotte's over-night things were down in the car with Aunt Eleanor who said she would rather wait there than come into the hospital. She could not endure hospitals.

'Is Eleanor here? She's actually out there?'

'She drove me from the station but wouldn't come in. She said seeing two people would be too much of a strain. I'm staying overnight with her and I expect she'll bring me in again in the morning.'

'Don't do that, Shah. Go to Daniel and Alexander. I shall be home in the afternoon and I'll write a letter. I'll tell you all about it.'

As it turned out the operation was not as terrifying as Owen expected. He was so calm about it he wondered whether they had slipped a tranquilliser into his morning tea. Uncomfortable, yes, even painful at times but as the masked figure of Mr Ibrahim Badawi – who had started proceedings by shaking him firmly by the hand – bent over him and the sister, masked too, pursed her lips in concentration Owen felt his body was being intimately explored and tranquillised at the same time. He stiffened but that was not unpleasant. He would have liked to see Mr Badawi press the bladder, or whatever it was, that would send air up the catheter to inflate that little balloon. He supposed it would be like the little puffer the dentist used to clear the detritus after a drilling but it was impossible to see what was going on.

He was like the frog in Walton's *Compleat Angler*, who was threaded on a hook to be used as bait for catching pike. He had to be sewn up and treated, Walton said, 'as though you loved him' which were the words that really stuck in the mind. That was how Owen felt he was being treated, threaded up the artery, from groin to chest, with a fine tube as though Mr Badawi and the sister did indeed love him and he did not want to respond, as he felt impelled to, by crying out in agony.

Sooner than he expected he was being wheeled away and Mr Badawi was grinning and saying, 'You'll do, Mr Bark. Very nice.' As everyone in hospital had called Owen by his first name he assumed Mr Badawi's greater formality, like the handshake, came from his foreign background. Nice to know the old courtesies were being kept up in this way.

Owen had been too optimistic in saying he would be home that afternoon because he was kept in another night for observation. This meant that Charlotte paid him another visit in the ward. Yes, he was fine. Everything had gone well. No complications. Not an experience one could undergo with a lot of dignity and he felt sore but the pain in his chest had gone. It was all quite miraculous really.

'Thank God,' said Charlotte. 'You've got your colour back.'

They talked of young Alex. Then Owen asked, 'How's that Czech boy?'

'You made a great impression. He talks about you a lot.'

Charlotte thought he had mentioned Tomas simply because he did not want to talk about himself. Owen was, though, interested in the boy and flattered by what Charlotte said. The implied praise was undeserved. Owen's gesture had been impulsive. He could see Tomas was caught up in a little storm he could not control and just had to throw him a lifeline. What really counted with Tomas was not that it came from this funny old man with his hesitant manner and sunken cheeks but that he was Charlotte's father. This conferred a special magic upon him. Owen knew all this without anyone having to tell him, as indirectly Charlotte had.

'I'd like to see him again. We might get on. How does he really see his future, I wonder.'

'Long term he'll go back to Prague. I've not any doubt about it. Because that is how he talks. He keeps in touch. That Bush House he works in seems to have a lot of information. The ice is breaking, he says, first in Poland and Hungary. Even in Prague.'

'So he doesn't want to go on with this college idea?'

'Things are not changing that quickly. Sure, he'll try to go to college.'

'Whatever happens I'd like him to meet Karl Strauss.'

He had quite taken to the boy but not really – he hesitantly admitted to himself – to the boy's father. Daniel seemed generous and undoubtedly loved Charlotte a great deal, all the more because she had presented him with Alexander. A lot could be forgiven him for that but not everything. Thrusting was the word Owen looked for. Ruthless too in his business dealings no doubt. He handled

Tomas clumsily, possibly the same way he handled those of his colleagues who were not in a position to fight back. Tomas could only fight back by running away. He would not run away from Charlotte, though, so he was bound to his father through this mother–substitute Owen sensed she had become. Daniel's pride in this bastard son did not spring out of any real generosity of spirit, it was just one aspect of his self-satisfaction and arrogance. At least, that is how Owen saw it. No mistake, though, Daniel's pride was something to be thankful for; he totally accepted the boy and would look after him, if only the boy would let him. So it turned on Charlotte.

A sister came and took Owen's temperature and blood pressure. Apparently both were satisfactory because she made one of those trained nurse remarks about his being an ideal patient and what a shame it would be he'd be leaving so soon when they had hardly got to know each other. A youth in a red track suit and plimsolls came round with trolley and offered them both tea and biscuits.

'I've got a confession to make,' said Charlotte.

He felt sure she was going to say something about the Reverend Michael Bellamy who had not pleased him with a sycophantic letter that made him wonder whether Charlotte was in the right hands; perhaps she was going to say that since she, Daniel and Alexander would be returning to the States before long there was not much point in going on with Bellamy anyway. But this was not the confession Charlotte was about to make.

'I've spoken to Meg in spite of what you said. I just had to. And it's quite right, it was her on the phone and she said you were both having a game. You knew who you were speaking to. It was sort of fun, she said.'

Owen could think of nothing effective to say about that. Just, 'Fun? Whatever can she mean?'

Fun? That was typical of Margaret. One of her complaints had been that he did not provide a lot of fun and she might have been right about that. She uttered the word as though it were written in capital letters, FUN, and made it sound strange, almost a mystery he would never rise to. The Hunt Ball came into the fun category. Odd though that she had never been to a Hunt Ball in her life. Why had he not spotted that before? But then it had been his dream not hers. The Hunt Ball was his fantasy. And yet he had never even ridden a horse! What Margaret had said on the telephone had not been fun at all and yet here she was taunting him with not seeing the joke.

'She said she couldn't believe you thought you were talking to me.'

'The telephone, well yes. I don't like it. I may not have been properly alert. I was just so relieved you were all right. No other thought in my head.'

'She just played you along. How do you like that? I think she is lying.'

'I hope you did not quarrel about it.'

'She was laughing too much. She just could not take it seriously.'

Charlotte keeping on good terms with her mother was more important than any satisfaction he might get from puzzling this all out to some conclusion. It might have been different if there had been any chance of meeting Margaret again. The only possibility of that would have been at the christening but now that Charlotte had decided this was to be back in the States any encounter was out. No doubt Margaret would attend. He would not. No position had to be prepared in advance. Just what kind of telephone conversation they'd had could be left unresolved.

'Lying? That's a bit hard, Shah. Why don't we leave it

all in the air. I can understand her believing what she says. It would be natural.'

'You're being very charitable.'

'I'm just admitting the possibility I was not quick witted enough to respond to her as she intended.'

He looked into those eyes which had been so black and tiny when he had first seen them and now were a grey-blue like Margaret's had been, so far as he could remember. What was it about Margaret? Oh, yes, that phone call in which she pretended to be Charlotte and said such hurtful things. It would just have to be overlooked. Perhaps it was a fudge but one had to live with fudges and contradictions. Even in the most profound matters of belief there were those most awful of contradictions to be held in balance. Lord, I believe. Help thou mine unbelief. Somewhere Margaret came into the argument over the womanliness of women but at the moment he could not quite see how. Or Eleanor, for that matter. Charlotte, on the other hand, he could see with perfect clarity. She had come so belatedly into his life as a quite unexpected blessing. He had not expected her nor had he expected Alexander.

'The main thing,' said Charlotte, 'is I didn't want you to be hurt.'

'Oh, I'm tough, girl. Don't be concerned on my behalf. You probably think your mother does not need your love. But she does and I know you will always give it to her because that is what women do, they are better than men. I have gone on about that quite a bit in my time and used it as an argument for not ordaining them in the church. I'm not clever enough to argue well. I shall always romanticise about women and here you are, coming along, and giving me more food for my romancing to feed on. God bless you, Shah! I've been confirmed in my beliefs by coming to know you. Life has been good to me. I did not expect you. I did not expect Alexander. I don't think I deserve all this goodness.'

Charlotte looked into his face, taking in the details, his eyes, his wispy eyebrows, the recessed cheeks that threw his jaw into prominence, rather as though she was trying to impress them on her memory.

'Father, I shall try to tell Meg what you have said. I don't suppose she will understand but I shall do my best.'

'When you go, Shah, wherever you go to, I'd like you to know I'll always feel near you.'

She bent down and kissed him again.

St Ebbe's was a small college but it had a good cellar and for the annual great dinner, the Gaudy, a whole platoon of claret was summoned up by the Fellows; the uncorked bottles stood shoulder to shoulder on the white-draped side-tables a good two hours before the diners took their place and the Master made his entrance. It had always irked Owen that the wine was not properly decanted but he had never succeeded in persuading anyone else of the need. The white wine was bought locally, plunged into the lead-lined Victorian coolers and stirred in the ice from time to time by the Chief Steward.

Owen relished such details and was determined to be well enough to take his usual place at the Gaudy. The Master encouraged him by saying, with black central European humour, that if he passed out they would prop him up; then, at the end of the Gaudy, when all the speeches had been made, he would be borne on high out of the hall like the dead hero of some Jacobean tragedy.

'Like Hamlet,' said Owen.

'Precisely.' The Master had a thunderous laugh. More

than ever Owen was convinced the eminent geologist regarded him not as an individual but as a specimen, rather as he would look on a rock sample. A specimen of what? Folk who grappled with unreal religious problems, probably, and yet were capable of taking jokes about their own mortality. How right he was. Owen was indeed amused and sent his dinner jacket to be cleaned. His gown was ancient and a bit rusty but it would serve. He would put on a good show. He would talk as well as any of them and when it was all over he wanted people to go away saying, 'Owen Bark was on form tonight.'

An Emeritus could not invite guests or he would have asked Tomas. The boy would have sat at his side and been attentive to his needs. If the noise and rejoicing became too much for him Tomas, he knew, would have known what to do. He would pull his chair back, ease him to his feet and gently lead him out. But an invitation would have given Tomas too great an expectation of a college place. So instead of Tomas he had sitting on his right a young woman in an obviously new gown and with superbly dressed black hair, a junior fellow he gathered, who was working on – what was it? Chartism. How boring! Why such a beautiful young woman had time for a subject like Chartism remained beyond him. He was quite enchanted by her and her throaty voice. Old men could be passionate too.

'I can remember when there were no women at a Gaudy. Not so long ago either. Not even Fellows' wives. Now it seems quite natural for them to be there, and in their own right as academics. But I wonder whether women really take to the academic life.' There he was again, generalising about women. What did he really know about them? 'Do you think, Miss – '

'Dr Evanthe Moore,' she said. She actually turned her

188

head to look at him and he saw, with pleasure, how large and brown her eyes really were. 'Why do you think women are any different from men academically? Or in any other respect for that matter?'

When he was silent she said, 'I really do think I am entitled to an answer.'

'I used to think I had one but now I am not so sure.'

'Why, Mr Bark.' She had discovered his name. 'Whatever does that mean? You *used* to have an answer!'

'It was, very roughly, that women were better than men.'

She tinkled. 'And now you think they are not.'

'Experience has taught me they are much of a muchness.'

'In scholarship? In politics?'

Owen had been trying to eat his fish until this conversation started but now he could not go on because his hands seemed suddenly to be curiously heavy. He stared at the fish with his hands on the table before him as inert as the fish itself. He wanted to say he would always believe women had special gifts but he no longer saw them touched with magic. The *Courier* had dropped him but if he had still been writing that monthly article he would have avoided the ordination of women. He had campaigned against it not for doctrinal reasons – he had been clear about that from the beginning – but out of regard for what he thought real women were like or were capable of becoming. Margaret had taught him differently. His argument had grown out of a personal need, for finding not a priest but a lover.

This realisation made the ordination of women just too churchy a subject. Now he was on the brink of some larger insight. What did talk of God's goodness really mean? Wasn't it extraordinary that in spite of all the

189

evidence to the contrary belief in this goodness took such root? It was the expression of a deep need, deeper even than his own need for human love. At that very moment, with the Gaudy roaring all around him, he felt taken over. First his hands were numb. Then his legs. What could it be but the coming of the most profound reality of all, the embracing love of God?

The man on his left was, he gathered, a journalist, name of Green. He said, 'Excuse me, sir, I couldn't help hearing what you said. We've got a woman prime minister now, remember.'

'And the university snubbed her. They refused her an honorary doctorate.'

'That's their privilege, isn't it? If Mrs Thatcher sets the academics against her she must expect that sort of snub.'

Owen was fired up in spite of the creeping numbness. His voice remained all right. 'The university behaved disgracefully. I would never vote for Mrs Thatcher in an election but I have to say the university was wrong. They failed to recognise achievement.'

'Is there something the matter, sir?'

'Yes, I think there is.'

'Perhaps a sip of water?'

Owen felt the numbness creep from his limbs towards his heart. In spite of the conversation going on all around he could hear his heart beating, chirping as it went, like a bird in its nest. For some time he had been aware of a woman sitting opposite. Her face was familiar and yet strange. Her dress was strange too. Her academic gown half concealed a jumper with that old familiar Mickey Mouse. But it must have been an illusion because this woman was leaning towards him with a raised glass.

'I drink to your health,' she said. She was no stranger. She was Charlotte whom he had last seen when she and

Daniel brought Alexander to say goodbye before leaving for New York. Dear Alexander! To think he would live on into a new century. But why was Charlotte there? She was gentle, she was kind, she was to be a Christian and she loved him. What a great, late gift that was. He had made his will. Everything went to her in the expectation it would all go to Alexander in time. Then Charlotte's face changed and became her mother's. Margaret looked just as she had when bound for the Hunt Ball on the deck of the QE2, radiant and happy.

'Drink this,' she said, offering the wine, 'in memory of me.'

Owen cried out, the conversation died and other faces were turned in his direction. Dr Evanthe Moore stood up. He had seen fear in the wine. Margaret was offering him not just a cup but his past life.

The journalist said, 'You're very hot, sir. Let me loosen your tie and unbutton your collar.'

It was an ordinary black tie and dress shirt, no clerical collar, so there was no difficulty in doing what Green offered. Owen was impatient to be gone from the Gaudy though. It had all proved too much for him and he had been foolish to come. Out there the sun was shining on the flowery summer fields. There was a lady with a bright sky of fleecy clouds behind her. She held a sunshade with a green lining so that her face was in shadow. In a little while he would see that face more clearly. He was stepping at last into the painting Eleanor had never properly been told about and so had always been his own.